Practical Web Traffic Analysis:

Standards, Privacy, Techniques, Results

Peter Fletcher

Alex Poon

Ben Pearce

Peter Comber

© 2002 glasshaus

Published by glasshaus Ltd,
Arden House,
1102 Warwick Road,
Acocks Green,
Birmingham,
B27 6BH, UK

Printed in the United States
ISBN 1-904151-18-3

Practical Web Traffic Analysis:

Standards, Privacy, Techniques, Results

Cover Image

James Chew is currently studying Multimedia Computing in Melbourne, Australia. Graphic Design started out just as a hobby, but quickly grew to become somewhat of an obsession in extending his knowledge and skills. Apart from design, James plays guitar and draws inspiration from music. James also enjoys designing, and redesigning his website *http://chewman.plastiqueweb.com* which is an online folio of work he has done.

James can be contacted via his website or through e-mail, *chewman@studiowhiz.com*.

glasshaus

labor-saving devices for web professionals

© 2002 glasshaus

Trademark Acknowledgements

glasshaus has endeavored to provide trademark information about all the companies and products mentioned in this book by the appropriate use of capitals. However, glasshaus cannot guarantee the accuracy of this information.

eBay™ screenshots used by permission of eBay™ Inc.

BBC News is a trademark of the British Broadcasting Corporation and is used under license. Screenshots and logos used by permission of the BBC.

ASPToday screenshots used by permission of ASPToday.

Credits

Authors
Peter Fletcher
Alex Poon
Ben Pearce
Peter Comber

Additional Material
SmartGirl.org
The Onion
NYTimes.com

Technical Reviewers
Dick Bennett
Jon Duckett
Richard Foan
Mark Horner
Tim Luoma
David Wertheimer

Proof Reader
Agnes Wiggers

Commissioning Editors
Peter Fletcher
Amanda Kay

Technical Editors
Mark Waterhouse
Alessandro Ansa

Managing Editor
Liz Toy

Publisher
Viv Emery

Project Manager
Sophie Edwards

Production Coordinators
Pip Wonson
Rachel Taylor

Cover
Dawn Chellingworth

Cover Image
James Chew

Indexer
Bill Joncocks

About the Authors

Peter Comber

It is nearly seven years since Pete Comber started working with the Internet. Having just started working in direct marketing, like most junior execs he quickly became frustrated with the fragile, incomplete, and temperamental customer databases upon which the ambitious DM strategies tended to exist. With the Internet boom in the late 1990s, he became convinced that there was massive potential for the Internet to provide large volumes of data not just about what people purchased, but about what they looked at, what they discarded, and potentially granting some insight into how people came to make their buying decisions. Having analyzed Internet data for four years for the UK's biggest motoring web site, he joined the BBC at the end of 2001 in the hope that would be able to provide some useful insights into how people use the BBC News Online service.

Peter Fletcher

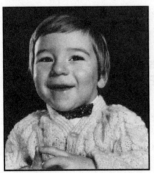

Peter Fletcher has been working in web development since 1997, via a degree in Philosophy and Theatre Studies and an MSc in Cognitive Science. Interests, professional and recreational, include using the Web as a distributed communications medium, analyzing web traffic data, and working with experimental performance group Stan's Cafe. His personal projects are documented at *www.joyfeed.com*. He is now a freelance web consultant and writer, dividing his time between Birmingham and Barcelona.

Ben Pearce

There's plenty about me later on, so I'd like to just say some thank-yous...

I would firstly like to thank Pete Fletcher for giving me the opportunity to talk about my work in this book. I hope it is useful and interesting reading for you.

I would also like to thank my wonderful wife Ange for all her support (not to mention the cakes!), and of course Jesus Christ who is my inspiration in everything.

Alex Poon

Alex Poon, originally from Baton Rouge, Louisiana, now lives with his wife Buffy and son Tyler in Northern California. He has a PhD from Stanford University. He was one of the first engineers at eBay, and started off as the de facto "UI guy" back in 1997. He started eBay's first user-interface group at eBay in 1999, then later ran the Advanced Technologies Group, during which his team implemented eBay's first web analytics system. Although Alex recently left eBay after five years, the company was happy to have him describe its analytics process in his own words.

To Buffy, who means everything to me.

Table of Contents

Table of Contents

Web Traffic Analysis
Introduction

Knowing how much traffic your site gets, and which parts get more than others, can be vitally important to understanding what visitors are getting from your site. With a bit of analysis of your server logs, you could discover that people are using your site in a way you didn't expect. Once you get a better idea of usage patterns for your site, you can begin to work on ironing out any problem areas such as that page that most shoppers never get beyond.

So, if you've ever wondered how to find out which day of the week your site gets most visits, this is the book for you. In fact if you've ever wondered how much traffic your site gets, then this is definitely the book for you. In the coming pages we look at the most important aspects of analyzing web traffic, including a comprehensive discussion of the key terms and their usage.

What's it all About?

To get the full benefit from *Chapter 1*, there are things you should know before we get there. You'll have noticed that we didn't say "If you want to know how many people have visited your site, this is the book for you," and with good reason. As we'll learn in *Chapter 1*, we can't really know this mystical figure for a number of reasons. Chiefly, because the site is accessed via HTTP which only recognizes requests for information and doesn't maintain a connection with a visitor, we can at best only get an indication of how many people have visited the site in any given time period. Instead, it has become widely accepted that a different figure be used, one which we can measure accurately, and that is the number of page requests.

In fact, this is all we can really measure with any hope of accuracy – pretty much everything else is extrapolation and educated guesswork.

Don't worry that you won't be able to tell your advertisers that you don't know how many people visit your site each day, because they shouldn't be expecting you to tell them. They should be interested in how many page impressions your site generates per day, and with a little help from this book you'll be able to tell them.

Despite having said that there is only one thing we can measure with real accuracy, there are a number of other elements to analyzing your web traffic. The first of these is knowing where to find evidence of your traffic, and how to interpret it. As we'll see, initially in *Chapter 1* but also throughout the book, this information comes to you in the form of log files generated by the web server hosting your site. Every time the server receives a request for a page, be it a simple HTML file, a picture, or a dynamic server-side scripting file, it makes a record of the request. This record includes the date and time of the request, where it came from, the file requested, and the manner in which it was requested. Importantly, if there was a cookie involved in the request, the name of the cookie is recorded as well. Counting the unique cookies in each log is as close as we get to knowing how many people visited the site – not everyone accepts cookies in their browser, for a variety of reasons. Some people may visit the site from more than one computer, and some people may even use more than one browser on the same computer.

Once we have the log file, we need to know what to do with it. Rather than have someone with a pencil and some paper read through the whole thing tallying up the page impressions and unique cookies, there's a selection of software available to do the hard work for you. Some of this software is very expensive, and some of it, like the main tool we'll be using in this book, is so cheap it's free! Specifically, we'll be looking at how a tool called Analog can be used to interpret your web server's log files. If you feel up for a challenge, you could write your own log file analysis utility, a common choice. We'll be taking a look at how one of these works, the very one in fact that is used to analyze the log files for our own site, *http://www.glasshaus.com*.

Of course, as anyone who has done any research involving statistics will know, having some numbers doesn't mean you'll know what's happening. Interpretation, whether we like it or not, has some part to play, as well as application. In the selection of case studies that make up the second half of the book, we'll see some of the benefits that can be gleaned from in-depth analysis of your site traffic. If you know where people stop trying to pay for your products, you know where you should really improve your site.

Who is this Book for?

This book is for you if you need to learn more about web traffic analysis, whether you've been told to present some figures to wow the board or you've been told to get the figures so someone else can use them to wow the board. It's for people who want to know what to put in traffic reports, what you can know about your visitors, what you're not allowed to know, and of course how to get the information in the first place.

We're not going to assume that you know vast amounts about statistics, or are capable of hand-coding Amazon.com. What we do assume is an intermediate level of knowledge about the Web: basic scripting experience is useful for the technical parts, as is some familiarity with Access, and you'll need to know (or be prepared to learn) the basics of HTTP and how the Web works.

What do I Need to Begin?

For this book, a web site and access to its log files are a good start. Once you have your log files, you'll want to look at them with either Analog (*http://www.analog.cx/*), or the hand-built system available as part of the code download from *http://www.glasshaus.com*, which is built in Access 2000 (so you'll need a PC for those parts). We also use Excel 2000 for further analysis of the data from the hand-built system.

What's Inside?

As we've already seen, *Chapter 1* covers all the basics of web traffic analysis; from data analysis methods and theory to tools for log file analysis. If you find terms in later chapters that aren't explained there, *Chapter 1* is the place to look.

> *Reach is a common measure used in audience research, it measures the "market share" that any given site has claimed*

> *The server is unable to log where the user goes after leaving the site*

> *Applying standards and employing auditors is not a replacement for proper intelligent interrogation of the data being presented*

Chapter 2 takes a look at a hand-built web traffic analysis system, using Access 2000 and Excel 2000. We introduce the database in which log files are turned into easy-to-understand numbers, and look at how the information that goes in there is gathered, including setting cookies.

> *One of the key facets of this database solution is the ability of the analyst or administrator to specify exactly which data are required.*

> *The general principles that it exemplifies can be applied to almost any database and coding solution*

Chapter 3 tackles the thorny issue of privacy – it's all very well being able to track a visitor across your site, but some of the ways of doing this invade their privacy, and can expose us to legal problems. As well as examining what laws there are to be aware of, we talk about some real sites and discuss their privacy policy and how it impacts their gathering of web traffic metrics.

Chapters 4, *5*, and *6* are case studies, in which the people responsible for web traffic analysis for three large sites explains how they gather their data, and what they do with it.

> *There is no single "correct" attitude towards cookies, the situation changes depending on the circumstances*

> *It is especially important to engender trust in the mind of the user*

In *Chapter 4*, Peter Comber tells us how the BBC monitors the traffic on their vast content site, *News Online* (*http://news.bbc.co.uk*). As well as the differences in size, we see how useful it is to have frequent access to traffic reports, and how they indicate which stories people are most interested in.

> We have learned that most "web metrics" - including page impressions - are extremely context sensitive.

> *There was an assumption that, as the archive of articles was both so rich and so large, there must be a huge number of page impressions drawn from this part of the site*

In *Chapter 5* Alex Poon gives us the low-down on how *eBay* (*http://www.ebay.com*) deal with their own unique problems. Since knowing when people stopped trying to buy something is vitally important to any commerce venture, eBay used detailed web traffic analysis to discover the usage patterns of their visitors.

> *For every page on the eBay site, we wanted the ability to see how users got to that page, and where users went after it.*

> *We found it cost-prohibitive to track every single page view from every single eBay user. Instead, we implemented a random sampling algorithm that tracks only one out of every 100 users to the eBay site*

Finally, in *Chapter 6*, Ben Pearce talks about the development of web traffic analysis for the *ASPToday* site (*http://www.asptoday.com*), from its inception in February 1999 to the site's latest version in August 2002. Here we gain an insight into the ways that web traffic analysis can help to drive the redevelopment of a site.

> *The site depends upon accurate intelligence to inform the key business decisions that have influenced its evolution from a simple static web site to a dynamic e-commerce application.*

> *Learning from early experiences of log analysis, the technical team and business team worked together to determine what information was required*

Support and Feedback

Although we aim for perfection, the sad fact of book publication is that a few errors will slip through. We would like to apologize for any errors that have reached this book despite our best efforts. If you spot an error, please let us know about it using the e-mail address *support@glasshaus.com*. If it's something that will help other readers, then we'll put it up on the errata page at *http://www.glasshaus.com*.

This e-mail address can also be used to access our support network. If you have trouble running any of the code in this book, or have a related question that you feel the book didn't answer, please mail your problem to the above address quoting the title of the book (*Practical Web Traffic Analysis*), the last 4 digits of its ISBN (**1183**), and the relevant chapter and page number.

Web Support

You'll want to go and visit our web site, at *http://www.glasshaus.com*. It features a freely downloadable compressed version of the code for this book, in both `.zip` and `.sit` formats. You can also find details of all our other published books, author interviews, and more.

1

- Theory and terminology

- Guidelines - what you can measure

- Using Analog

Author: Peter Fletcher

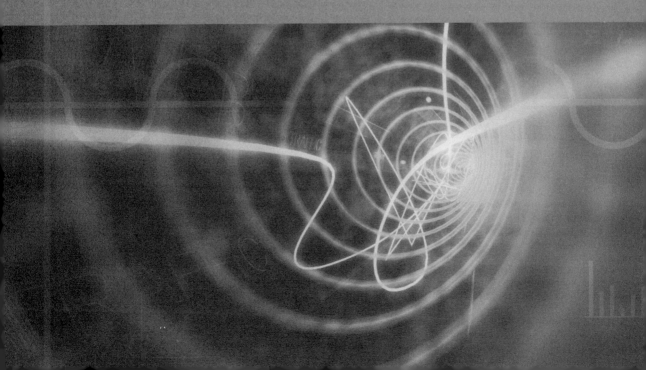

Analytics Techniques

We want to know who is coming to our web site, whether they have been here before, where they came from, what they are looking at, what route they take through the site, how long they spend on each page, and why they leave. Which, if any, of these objectives are possible?

In this chapter, we will define the landscape of Web Traffic Analysis, beginning with the various methods available to us, followed by a discussion of some of the advantages and disadvantages of these methods. Then we go back to basics, and determine exactly what it is that we can know, and what we cannot know, and the extent to which it is safe to make some assumptions. Having established these principles, we examine the emerging standards for web traffic analysis, and discuss whether there are any good "rules" that we should follow.

Comparative Overview of Analysis Methods

There are three broad types of web traffic analysis, defined by the source of the data that is being recorded and analyzed. These are data collected from activity on the web server, data collected from panel surveys, and data collected from the client or browser using "tags" or "web bugs". We can look at these in turn to determine their relative merits.

Server Logs

The web server logs all of the files that are requested from it, and these logs can be parsed and analyzed using custom software, or a variety of applications, either as free software or proprietary solutions. The logging can either be performed by the web server itself, with the data stored in a log file, or the web site could use custom software to record requests made directly into a database.

Advantages

● The information contained in the log file is very rich. Every request made of the server is recorded in the log, and these requests contain a large amount of data. This data can be mined to reveal patterns of activity including the most popular parts of the site, the demand over time, and information about the users making the request.

● The web site owns and controls the data. The log file only contains a record of the requests made to the web server, and the information is completely in the control of the site's owners; a situation that does not necessarily exist with other solutions, such as panel surveys or outsourced solutions.

● Very useful for assessing the load on the server. Log files can be set to record the volume of data being transferred, which requests were unsuccessful, and other functions useful to system administrators and site designers. Heavy use of large files and repeated failure codes might indicate an area of excessive load, or poorly usable or broken, parts of the site.

Disadvantages

*The time and sequence of the pages viewed on the site is known as the **click-stream***

● The information is incomplete. As this method only records server requests, any activity that does not reach the server will not be recorded. This principally includes files cached by the user's ISP, company proxy server, or browser. It's also not possible to determine click-stream data, such as the amount of time spent on each page.

● The data includes a lot of noise. Basic log file analysis must identify and remove traffic that artificially inflates the "real" traffic figures. This includes requests made by robots (such as Google), and requests that were unsuccessful (those returning a "404", for example). It might also be desirable to filter the analysis of actual files being requested, for example ignoring requests for image files and stylesheets.

● Individual user information is misleading. As HTTP allows users to access files anonymously, the server will only record the IP address of the machine making the request. In the case of many ISPs or company proxy servers, these IP addresses can represent large numbers of individual users.

Sometimes, and particularly with high volume sites, the sheer amount of data can be an obstacle in itself; wading through the mass of information and filtering out the noise can be daunting. If not done with great care, it can adversely affect the accuracy of the results.

Conclusion

Analyzing the server logs is probably the most common form of traffic analysis, but it is fraught with difficulties. The very density and magnitude of the data contained in log files can be misleading, as robots, caching, and multi-user IP addresses cloud the picture. There are many log file analysis tools available that promise to cut through the fog, but in practice the information that these tools provide is often ambiguous, and potentially highly misleading in the hands of those who do not understand how the information presented has been derived from the raw data.

While log files provide the most widely accessible means for web traffic analysis, they also potentially pose the most problems. For this reason, we will look at log file analysis in more detail later on in this chapter, explaining exactly what a log file can and cannot tell us, and look at how one particular tool, the free software Analog, attempts to avoid the pitfalls inherent in normal log file analysis.

Panel Surveys

A research company randomly selects volunteers to be part of a panel of users, designed to represent the Internet-using population. The company installs tracking equipment on the volunteers' home computers, and this records all of the Internet activity in the household. The system works in a similar way to that which determines television-viewing figures, and is useful in much the same way. Companies that provide these sorts of services include MMXI, NetValue, and NetRatings.

Advantages

- The data collected is very accurate for each particular computer in the survey. Individual users can identify themselves, but there is no guarantee that this is done accurately every time. The equipment that records activity will detect every request made, and all data uploaded and downloaded, surmounting common problems normally presented by the caching of files, or use of browser functions such as the *Back* button. This method will also detect information such as the time spent viewing each page, giving a very clear picture of the click-stream patterns of the users.

- The same criteria and definitions are used for all sites. As there is no need to make assumptions about "visits", "unique users", or other constructs that inevitably imply a margin of error that is magnified when comparisons are made between different sites, such comparisons are on safer ground.

- Though anonymous, each piece of data can be linked to specific users. This enables very accurate demographic information to be recorded, and makes it possible to track the "reach" of each site: how well the site has penetrated into the population of Internet users. This is important for sites that are looking to broaden their appeal to a wide audience (as opposed to targeting a specific market and focusing resources exclusively there).

Reach is a common measure used in audience research. Put simply, it measures the "market share" that any given site (or channel, or product), has claimed within a given population. We will see later how the BBC uses Reach to determine what proportion of the Internet-using British public has accessed their sites in a given month. Reach is different from measures such as "Users" or "Visits", in that it is measuring the proportion of a population, rather than counting individual items.

- There are no privacy issues with the collection of the data because all users are volunteers, and the information is aggregated and anonymous.

Disadvantages

- These types of surveys are predominantly of home use only. As much Internet use takes place outside of the home, mainly at the workplace, this is a serious limitation. The figures are likely to be skewed towards more domestic activities. It is highly likely that usage patterns differ widely between the home and the office, not only by which sites are visited, but also the pattern of behavior: for example, fleeting and sporadic visits to sites at work, compared with more in-depth and concerted use for a sustained period while at home.

- The sample is to a degree self-selecting, as all participants are volunteers. It is possible that, even with very sophisticated selection procedures, usage patterns for those willing to sign up to the survey will differ from those who do not. This problem is compounded by the fact that users know they are being monitored (albeit anonymously), and might regulate their surfing habits accordingly.

- There are statistical errors inherent in the sampling process. By definition, the survey contains only a small fraction of the overall population of Internet users, and some degree of error will be introduced as the figures for the survey are extrapolated. This problem is exacerbated by the fact that different panels do not use the same figure for the size of the overall population, making comparisons of the scaled data between panels unreliable.

- Extrapolating information about smaller sites is not reliable. As data is collected from a relatively small sample, and then scaled up, the margin for error is too high for reliable analysis for all but the largest sites.

Conclusion

Panel survey research should probably be viewed as only applicable for certain purposes, and for certain sites, such as large sites aimed predominantly at domestic users. The information it gathers is not reliable for any but the largest sites, due to the margin of error implicit in the small sample. However, as a way for the largest sites on the Web to track the numbers and demographics of their users (and compare themselves to their competitors' audited figures), it can be a valuable tool.

Browser Analysis: Tagging or Web Bugs

This is a relatively new method of traffic analysis, in which client-side script (referred to as a "tag" or "web bug" – hereafter "tag" for short) designed to run in the user's browser each time the page is loaded, is inserted on each page on the web site. This method is intended to circumvent problems with server log analysis such as the caching of pages, because the script runs on the client and makes a request every time the page appears in the browser.

There are two ways in which this is commonly implemented. First, the page simply contains an image tag for a 1x1 GIF, which the server will record when requested in the usual way. Second, the page contains JavaScript code that will also make a request for the 1x1 GIF. The JavaScript method is a little more robust, as it will attempt to call download the file every time the page is loaded. Not all browsers support client scripting, however, so the best implementations actually make use of both methods. This sort of solution is often outsourced to companies specializing in data collection and analysis, and they have often developed techniques for ensuring that browsers or ISPs do not cache their one-pixel files.

Advantages

- Since this method typically employs "cache-busting" techniques – ensuring that the one-pixel image is downloaded every time, then – while not foolproof – some of the problems of caching for server logs are not present. Perhaps the primary claim in favor of tagging is that it is able to register all views of each page, with requests coming directly from the script on the page. As a consequence of this, the system records real user behavior, such as the click-stream. In particular, tagging removes the uncertainty generated by use of the Back button, which loads a page in the browser window, but will not normally send a new request to the server, as the browser will use its own, cached version of the page instead.

- Other information about the user can be recorded. Script in the tag can pick up other useful items such as the time zone settings of the user's clock – from which geographical location can be inferred (although this might raise privacy alarm bells, so it is best treated with caution). Also, by sending information as the page exits, it is possible to determine the destination of the user as they leave the site.

- Tagging solutions are typically outsourced. There are some clear benefits to keeping this sort of analysis as an outsourced solution: using experts means the system can be put in place quickly and efficiently, and the process is reliable, stable, and scalable.

- The tagging system can be extended beyond web pages. Any device that understands the scripting tag can be tracked, for example, placing a tag in an HTML e-mail can give excellent feedback on the number of users that actually opened each mail, and what they did next.

Disadvantages

- Privacy concerns. Executing script that has the ability to detect information about the user and their activity raises some serious privacy concerns. For example, the ability to detect the destination of a user once they leave your site is problematic, as the user might legitimately claim that, once they have left your site, their following destination is, quite literally, none of your business. Discussion of what HTTP requests you should consider your business follows in the next section, and we will look at privacy issues in much more detail in *Chapter 3*.

- Every item needs to be tagged. On a web site, only tagging a few pages will render any (click-stream) data collected virtually useless, so every single page must be tagged. Depending on the architecture of the site, and design decisions made previously (such as the use of server-side includes) this could be an insurmountable task. Tagging will also inevitably add "weight" to the page, as the script has to run each time, connecting to the server, and collecting the GIF. Even if the size of the file is small, a round trip is a round trip.

- The costs of outsourcing. While handing over the management of this solution to a third party has advantages, it also has a financial downside. This is perhaps more acute for high traffic sites, as the load that their users will place on the third party will be considerable, and this will inevitably play a part in the pricing of the solution. Later in the book, we will see how eBay managed to mitigate this problem with some clever scripting of their own.

- Ownership and access to the data. The outsourcing process can lead to ambiguities in the ownership of the data, and often the data is, in fact, owned by the third party. In addition, access to the data can be difficult, as the web site will not have as much control over the information and its analysis as would be the case if the whole process remained in-house.

- The system will not work for those who do not have JavaScript enabled, or are using a non-JavaScript browser, such as Opera.

Conclusion

Tagging could prove a viable means of accurately tracking real user behavior, but there are a number of issues with it as a complete solution at the moment. Not all web sites are in a position to commit to an outsourcing company as this method usually requires, and privacy concerns remain a significant obstacle, as both users and legislators are becoming more suspicious of methods used to monitor our activity online.

The Skeptical Analyst

In this section, we will get to the root of what we can or cannot know by analyzing server log files – still by far the most popular method of tracking web traffic. We will look at exactly what is usually contained in a log file, what this can tell us, and what it is not possible to deduce from this data. Then we will look at what is probably the most widely used log file analysis tool, Analog, and examine how it takes a skeptical, though accurate, and brilliantly efficient, view of what the log file is telling us. Finally, we will look at cookies, a widely used attempt to add some detail to server log analysis, and try to determine the extent to which they are useful.

Log Files

First things first, what data is recorded in a log file? A web server such as Apache or Microsoft's IIS can be configured to record all requests received, and includes both information received in the HTTP request itself and information generated by the server, such as file size, and the status of the request (such as success or failure).

Each web server can be configured to record more or less information about each request, and it is up to the server administrator and the site manager (who might be the same person) to decide what data is relevant and what is not. In the example in this chapter, I have made a typical selection based on a judgment as to what is useful for the purposes of analyzing user behavior on a site, as well as some common log file elements. It is worth taking time now to go through this selection and explain what each element tells us. The information below is taken from a log file.

date time

As it sounds, this indicates the time and date of the request. This is set to the time and date on the server hosting the site, which is likely to be the local time, UTC, or GMT – make sure you know which.

c-ip

This is the IP address of the computer – the client – making the request. However, this is not necessarily the IP address of the end user's computer, and it is likely to be a company or ISP proxy server. There are a number of issues with making assumptions about the client IP address, which we discuss later.

s-ip

Here we have the IP address of the server receiving the request. Hopefully this will come as no surprise, but it is included here as it is a standard entry in most log files. Also, depending on the architecture of the hosting system, several different servers may be used, and this field is helpful to determine which one this log file belongs to. Each web server produces its own log file, so load-balanced installations generate several files which need to be collated.

s-port

This is the port through which the request was received. Standard HTTP requests are typically received on port 80.

cs-method

Here's the method of the request. Most HTTP requests are made using the GET method, but they can also be made using POST (typically for web form data), or various less common methods.

cs-uri-stem

The part of the URI requested after the domain name. For example, a request for the glasshaus web site home page: *http://www.glasshaus.com/default.asp* would appear as "*/default.asp*".

cs-uri-query

The query string data from the requested URI.

sc-status

The status of the request, for example whether it succeeded, was refused, file could not be found, and so on. For the purposes of traffic analysis, it is advisable to ignore log entries with certain status codes. We will discuss this in more detail later.

cs(User-Agent)

This is effectively the type of browser used to make the request, though this would also include automated systems such as search engine robots. The following line is typical, indicating that the user agent was a Mozilla 4.0+ compatible browser (in fact Internet Explorer 6.0) running on Windows NT 5.0 (or Windows 2000 to its friends):

```
Mozilla/4.0+(compatible;+MSIE+6.0;+Windows+NT+5.0)
```

A word of warning here: a user agent can claim to be whatever it likes, and this is not "verified" by the server. For example, some browsers claim to be Internet Explorer 5.0, in order to circumvent the practice of certain web pages to check which browser is requesting the page, and if it is too "obscure", return a message advising the user to "upgrade their browser".

cs(Cookie)

Any cookie data that is included in the request. We will be taking an in-depth look at the extent to which cookies are useful to us later on.

cs(Referer)

If the request was initiated by clicking on a link from a source which has a URI, then that URI appears here as the "referer". Amusingly, this misspelling (it should be referrer) is in the original HTTP specification, and has remained there ever since. We'll use the correct spelling.

Usually, the vast majority of referrers in the log will be from the web site itself, indicating that users are accessing pages using the web site's own internal linking. Due to caching and other effects, it is unsafe to assume that this represents a reliable click-stream, but this field is potentially interesting as an indication of which external sites are driving our traffic. The URI is recorded in full, including the query string data, which is useful as it indicates the search terms used when the referrer is a search engine.

W3C links:
For a full list of the HTTP methods, visit *http://www.w3.org/Protocols/HTTP/Methods.html*
The W3C has a full list of status codes here: *http://www.w3.org/Protocols/rfc2616/rfc2616-sec10.html*
More information is available on HTTP referrer here:
http://www.w3.org/Protocols/rfc2616/rfc2616-sec14.html#sec14.36

What Does the Log Not Tell Us?

The temptation, with so rich a source of data as a log file, is to read too much into it, but the information in a log file is likely to be incomplete and misleading. We will examine here the skeptical case against making assumptions based on the data in a log file. Later in this chapter we look at the case in favor of intelligent assumptions, and in particular the advocacy of standards for web analysis. First, we need to understand exactly where the traps are.

Users in the Log File are Anonymous

> *IP addresses remain useful for giving an impression of which types of organization are accessing your web site, but for identifying individual users they are effectively useless.*

HTTP is an anonymous and stateless protocol. This means that users are not individually identifiable, and each request made is independent and not explicitly connected to other requests by the same user (unless the web site requires a password login, for example, or uses some other method of state-management, such as cookies). The server does know the IP address of the computer making the request (so that it knows where to send the response), but this IP address does not necessarily relate to a single unique user for two reasons:

- Firstly, as mentioned previously, ISP, university, or company proxy servers or firewalls will often use a single IP address to represent several users.

- Secondly, some ISPs can allocate a different IP address to a user for each request.

Finding a way out of this predicament of over- and under-counting with any degree of certainty is difficult. IP addresses remain useful for giving an impression of which types of organization are accessing your web site, but for identifying individual users they are effectively useless.

This means that we cannot deduce how many unique users we have had. It also means that we cannot deduce how many "visits" we have had. A "visit" or "session" is often used to describe a connected sequence of requests from a single unique user. Clearly, as it is not possible to determine unique users from the IP address alone, attaching requests to them and compiling them into a single session is also a meaningless activity. Cookies are often cited as a realistic way to get around the problem of identifying users, but they are fraught with difficulties of their own, and we cannot assume that they provide a foolproof system of user identification. They are, however, very extensively deployed, so we will look at them in detail later in this chapter.

Even with the assumption that in certain cases this was possible, how do we define a distinct visit? What length of gap between page requests can we reasonably assume constitutes a new visit: ten minutes, thirty minutes, an hour, twenty-four hours? In practice, visits vary in length, sometimes users will not request a page for a long time, but will still consider themselves to be visiting the site. Perhaps they have taken time out to answer an e-mail or the telephone, or fix a snack? They may even be paying close attention to the site all along, reading a longer article in detail. Add to this the issue highlighted above that not all requests actually get logged in the first place, and we can see that allocating a meaningful "time-out" period for the purposes of defining visits is almost impossible.

Log File Data is Incomplete

The server can only record the requests that it receives. When a user clicks on a link to request a page from our web site, that request may never reach the server, as the files requested might be cached by the browser, or the user's ISP or company proxy server. This has a number of effects. The log will be undercounting the "real" number of page impressions that our site is generating, and this will generally penalize the more popular pages on the site, as these are the ones most likely to be cached.

The fact that the log is incomplete makes assumptions about the user's actual route through the site highly problematic (even assuming that we can identify individual users). It is common practice to use the *Back* button to navigate around a site, viewing a page, and then going back a step, perhaps to an index, and then viewing another page. By using the *Back* button (an excellent usability tool incidentally) in this way, popular pages, and in particular "index" pages which contain navigational links, will often be undercounted, presenting us with a false "click-stream". Nevertheless, much analysis of log files incorrectly assumes that they contain a complete picture of user activity.

It is possible to design a web site that contains pages that instruct client machines not to cache them, and this is sometimes advocated as a potential solution to the problem of incomplete log data. This is, however, probably not advisable. Caching is there for a reason: to improve the user experience by speeding up download times, and to reduce strain on the web server. While there are legitimate reasons why a designer might wish a web page not to be cached, for example on the homepage of a frequently updated news site, collecting traffic data is probably not one of them, and in any case, due to sophisticated caching techniques by ISPs, the data collected would still most likely be partly incomplete. It is better to know that the data is incomplete, and handle it accordingly, than to incorrectly assume that it is authoritative.

What Else Don't We Know?

Log files will not tell us how long a user has spent on the web site, or how long they spent viewing each page. Certainly we know the time of each request logged, but as we now realize, this is an incomplete picture of their route through the site. Even if it were possible to assume that the log recorded all requests, it cannot record the time at which the user stopped looking at the last page, or left the site for another.

The server is unable to log where the user goes after leaving the site, as by definition that request is sent to a different server. Time spent on the last page of the visit is unknown, and therefore the total time spent on the site cannot be determined. The possibility that the last page viewed might well be the one that held the attention of the user the longest can only add to this uncertainty. Certain sites, such as online banks, enforce a session log-in/off, but this does not tell us how long the final page was truly viewed for, as commonly users will allow the last page to time out, or simply close down the browser window. In any case, this solution is not appropriate for most sites.

> *if we define exactly the boundaries of what we know, then we can also define what we do not know, and that information becomes all the more valuable as a result.*

There are many commercial web analysis tools on the market that generate information on visits, unique users, time spent on each page, and so on. The problem with using one of these "off-the-peg" tools is that, without knowing how they work out these figures, and what assumptions they have made, it is difficult to assign any credibility to their results. Skeptical analysts are therefore suspicious of tools that claim to know too much, as they may be misleading at best, and at worst, plain wrong.

What Can We Say for Certain?

The skeptical view presented here may appear somewhat negative: if there are so many difficulties and ambiguities, why bother to analyze server logs at all? The answer here is that, if we define exactly the boundaries of what we know, then we can also define what we do not know, and that information becomes all the more valuable as a result. We will now look at the positive side to server log analysis, and determine what we can safely deduce, using the popular log analysis tool Analog.

Analog

Analog is an excellent tool for analysis for a number of reasons:

For more details about how this works in practice, and any restrictions of reuse, refer to the license that is included in the standard Analog download, or on the Web here: http://www.analog.cx/docs/Licence.txt.

- It is open source, free software. Any organization, large or small, rich or poor, can download and use it. It also means that, as open source software, more experienced developers can examine how it works, verifying its methodology, and adding extensions or adaptations. It also has versions to run on most platforms, including Windows, Mac, Linux, and Unix.

- The documentation is very explicit about what it does and does not do. The skeptical analyst viewpoint defined above has in part been derived from the rules to which Analog adheres: it does not make assumptions about the data that it collects, but merely reports the facts, as it finds them.

- The program is very efficient, and can process a large amount of data in a short period of time. Analog's creator, Stephen Turner, claims that it can process 28 million lines in 20 minutes, on a 266MHz chip (1Gb of data every five minutes). This makes Analog a practical application for even the highest volume sites.

As Analog is so strict in terms of what it allows into its reports, it also makes an excellent tool for understanding the mechanics of log files themselves. To web developers who are accustomed to using sophisticated GUI tools for creating web sites (which is, let's face it, most of us), Analog's text interface can seem intimidating and austere.

We should not be put off by this, however, because it is in fact very straightforward to set up and operate, and once the basic rules of the configuration file are established, very easy to customize to your own requirements.

The latest copy of Analog, with full documentation, can be downloaded from the Analog web site, at *http://www.analog.cx*. The download contains a copy of the program which is ready to run, and does not require any setup or installation. All that is required is that the configuration file, *analog.cfg*, has all the details entered into it, including the location of the log files to be analyzed. These files must be on the same computer that is running Analog, and so may need to be downloaded from the web server and placed in a suitable location. In practice, many of these administration functions can be run automatically, but for clarity here we will step through the process manually.

We can now take a look at how Analog can be used to analyze a log file, and examine what it claims to do.

Configuring Analog involves editing a simple text file. First, we need to specify where the log file to be analyzed is located:

```
LOGFILE C:\analog\logfiles\logfile.log
```

Analog returns the output in an HTML file, so we need to specify what we want this to be called, and we can choose to insert the name of the site (or part of the site) being analyzed:

```
OUTFILE report.html
HOSTNAME "My Website"
```

Analog counts all requests that have valid status codes. As far as Analog is concerned, this means codes in the 200's, and code 304 (a file is requested, but the file is not physically served, as the client already has a copy which has not been altered since it was previously cached). Full explanations for the decisions that Analog makes here are included in the supporting documentation, but in summary, it only counts genuine successful requests.

Unless we specify otherwise, Analog will count all files as requests, including images, stylesheets, and so on. This is fine so far as it goes, but we also need to know how many "pages" were downloaded. To do this, we need to tell Analog what we consider to be a viewable "page", as opposed to a file. We can do this either by listing all of the URIs for all of the pages that we want included, or by using wildcards to indicate the form that our pages take.

The simplest way to do this, assuming our site architecture is consistent with it, is to specify which file types to include. For example:

```
PAGEINCLUDE *.asp
PAGEINCLUDE *.pdf
PAGEINCLUDE *.htm
```

These lines indicate that all files with suffixes *.asp*, *.pdf* and *.htm*, should be counted as pages. Similarly, we can specify pages by directory. Any number of lines can be added to specify exactly what should be considered a page:

```
PAGEINCLUDE /articles/*
PAGEINCLUDE /default.asp
```

Analog uses this information to generate the general summary at the top of the report:

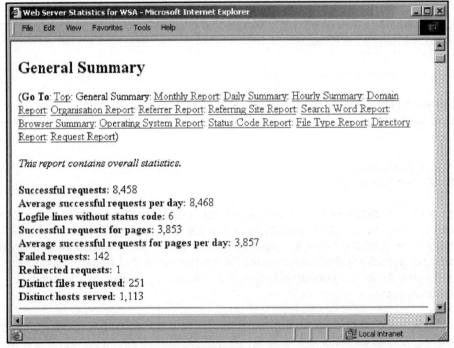

A typical general summary

It also uses it to generate a more detailed breakdown of the pages requested:

A request report, showing chart and list of most requested pages

We can tell Analog which user agents we want to exclude, robots for example. Any requests from a robot in this list will then not be counted as either a request, or a page. Telling Analog about robots is very straightforward:

```
ROBOTINCLUDE REGEXPI:robot
ROBOTINCLUDE REGEXPI:spider
ROBOTINCLUDE REGEXPI:crawler

ROBOTINCLUDE Googlebot*
ROBOTINCLUDE Infoseek*
ROBOTINCLUDE Scooter*
ROBOTINCLUDE Slurp*
ROBOTINCLUDE Ultraseek*
```

The first three lines above give Analog a regular expression instruction, essentially saying, "anything that says it is a robot or a spider or a crawler should be excluded". The other five lines name the specific known robots that we wish to exclude. Note that these instructions do not remove the relevant lines entirely, as we are interested in robot activity: we want to know what devices are accessing the site, but we don't want to confuse them with "genuine" page views.

Following on from this, we also want to tell Analog what we believe to be a search engine, so that it can report on the search words most commonly used to direct users to the site. Again, we can give Analog a named list:

```
SEARCHENGINE http://*altavista.*/* q
SEARCHENGINE http://*yahoo.*/* p
SEARCHENGINE http://*google.*/* q
SEARCHENGINE http://*lycos.*/* query
SEARCHENGINE http://*aol.*/* query
```

The first part of the line tells Analog that this is a search engine, the second part defines how to identify a referral from that search engine – basically the URL with wildcards – and the final part tells Analog how that particular site denotes the search words in its query string.

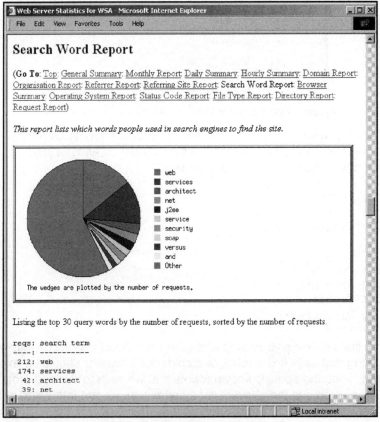

The search word report and chart

It is possible to turn the reporting of various elements on and off. For example, we can ask Analog to tell us about the referrers that have directed traffic to the site:

```
REFERRER ON
REFSITE ON
```

These two reports tell us which web pages have referred the most people to us, and which sites have referred the most, respectively:

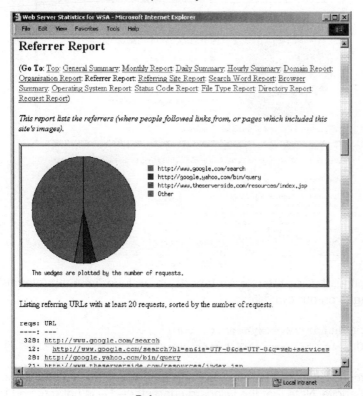

Referrer page report

Referrer site report

It is a good option, if using the referrer reports, to exclude "internal" referrals, that is those from pages on our own site:

```
REFREPEXCLUDE http://www.MyWebsite.com/*
REFSITEEXCLUDE http://www.MyWebsite.com/
```

The first command refers to the referring page report, and the second to the referring site report, as above. Note that the wildcard character – * – is not required in the case of the site report.

Another useful report is the browser summary, which is not included by default. As with many of the reports that Analog produces, there is an optional chart, but the basic report must be included for the chart to be displayed:

```
BROWSERSUM ON
BROWSUMCHART ON

SUBBROW */*
```

The last line here tells Analog to include a breakdown of each type of browser by version, which is rather useful, to avoid all versions of Internet Explorer being grouped together, for example. The output from the browser summary looks like this:

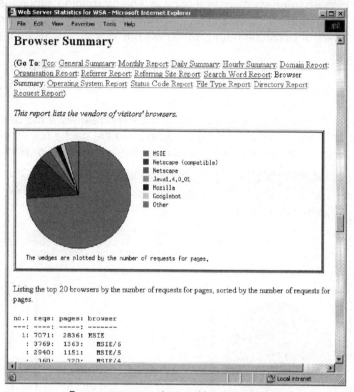

Browser summary chart and browser summary

The final element to note in the basic configuration file is the ability to create aliases for file extensions: essentially saying, "anything that ends with *.htm* is a HTML page, anything that ends with *.jpg* is a JPEG", and so on:

```
TYPEALIAS .html    ".html [Hypertext Markup Language]"
TYPEALIAS .htm     ".htm [Hypertext Markup Language]"
TYPEALIAS .jpg     ".jpg [JPEG graphics]"
TYPEALIAS .jpeg    ".jpeg [JPEG graphics]"
```

It is also possible to configure Analog to do a DNS lookup on the IP addresses in the log file, in other words turning 204.148.170.150 into *www.glasshaus.com*. This is useful for working out which organizations are accessing your site, and potentially also from which geographical location. Instructing Analog to perform a DNS lookup is easy: simply include the following command:

```
DNS WRITE
```

This instructs Analog to perform a DNS lookup of all the IP addresses in the logs being processed, and write a file called dnscache, which records details of the resolved addresses, for use next time. While Analog is running, it will also create a file called dnslock, which is there to prevent another copy of Analog running simultaneously from overwriting the information. dnscache is deleted once the processing is complete. There are three other types of DNS command, which will not look up any IP addresses:

- DNS NONE, which instructs Analog not to convert any IP addresses
- DNS READ, which only looks in the cache file, and does not perform any new lookups
- DNS LOOKUP, which will perform new lookups and reference the dnscache, but does not write the results of the new lookups into the cache file – this is used if DNS WRITE fails, for example if the dnscache file is locked by dnslock.

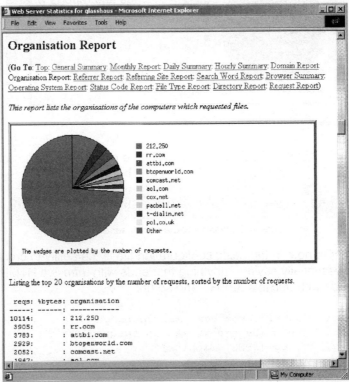

Organisation report, chart and summary

It is important to note that this is an extremely long process – in particular compared with the speed of Analog's normal operation. As an anecdotal illustration of the time involved, one of our log files that would normally be processed in less than 1 second took 39 minutes to complete the first time that DNS WRITE was set, because a new lookup had to be performed for all of the IP addresses in the file (over 600).

The second time it was run, however, was much quicker, as it could use the information in the cache file, and again completed in under a second. There are other applications, however, that are more optimized to perform DNS lookups in a more timely manner, and some of these are helpfully referenced in Analog's Helper Applications page: *http://www.analog.cx/helpers/*.

A word of caution here, however: as we have seen before, IP addresses conceal as much as they reveal, and it is dangerous to trust them too much. Many log files, for example, will reveal that a large proportion of users are accessing the site from Virginia, USA, but only because AOL hosts most of their proxy servers in that state. The actual users are distributed all over the country.

In summary, Analog is a great tool for conducting "skeptical analysis". It does not "interpret" the results that it finds in the logs, it parses and reports what is there. It does this very efficiently and accurately, and it is free software, which means that not only is it free of charge, but the source code is available for us to check and reconfigure if we so choose. As a starting point for web traffic analysis, Analog has a lot to recommend it, as it does its job without any fuss, and reminds us what information we know we know, and what information is the result of interpretation, valid or otherwise.

Cookies

As we have seen, ambiguities caused by the fact that HTTP is an anonymous and stateless protocol make it impossible to make reliable or accurate deductions about unique users and visits. For many web developers, the solution to this problem is the cookie. Now this humble confection has caused quite a bit of controversy recently, and we will be discussing privacy concerns in detail in Chapter 3. For the moment, we need to establish exactly what using cookies can tell us, and, as before, where the dangers in interpretation lie.

I have separated the discussion of cookies from that of how Analog acts as skeptical analyst. Though it is possible to include cookie data in the server logs, Analog does not explicitly have a report for this field, because cookies fail its test of reliability when it comes to interpreting the data. To understand why, we need to review how cookies work, how they can be used, and what assumptions we can make about the data they provide.

A cookie is a small text file, which is sent by the web server as part of the HTTP response. The cookie is stored by the user agent – in practice, the browser – and its contents are returned to the web server that sent it every time a new request is made to that server. There are various rules and security measures that accompany the use of cookies by the browser:

- The cookie data can only be returned to the server with the same domain that sent the original cookie. For example, the BBC can use a single cookie for all web sites that are part of the bbc.co.uk domain, including *www.bbc.co.uk*, *news.bbc.co.uk*, etc.

- Cookies can have an expiry date, which can be set well into the future. If no expiry date is set, then the cookie expires once the user closes down their browser. Cookies with expiry dates are sometimes referred to as "*permanent cookies*", and those without are referred to as "*session cookies*".

- The browser should allow the user to configure it to reject cookies, or regulate their acceptance, for example by warning when a site is offering to set a cookie.

Cookies therefore allow web developers and site administrators to place small quantities of data on the browser, which can be retrieved and used on future requests. This data is often designed to enhance seamlessly the user's experience, for example by recording preference settings that the user has opted for on a previous visit. Perhaps the most common use of a cookie, however, is to send a "**token**": a long randomly generated character string designed to uniquely identify that particular cookie, and by extension, that user. Each time the user makes a request to the web server, the token is sent, and this same token is returned in the cookie as part of the response.

This is an attempt to overcome the stateless nature of HTTP, as it effectively links all requests made by the same browser. It is possible to record the contents of the cookie in the log file, or a database, and count the number of distinct tokens, generating a figure for unique users to the web site. It is also possible to cross-reference all requests made with the same token, and construct data concerning visits. So why does Analog's documentation caution against counting cookies?

The answer is that, while it is possible to record and count this data, too many assumptions have to be made to go from "I have *x* number of distinct tokens in the log file" to "I have *x* number of unique users". There are several problems with these assumptions:

- Users can opt to reject cookies altogether. In this case, the browser will never send cookie data back to the server. Users that opt to do this are therefore invisible to this analysis.

- Cookies are set on browser instances, not people. It is possible, even likely, that a single individual might be represented by several different tokens for a given web site. For example, if they have two different types of browser on their machine (Netscape and Internet Explorer, say), and they use both browsers to visit the web site over a period of time, then they will appear in the web site's analysis as two different individuals.

Similarly, if someone visits a web site from two different machines, one at home and one at work, for example, then again, they will appear as two unique users (or more, if they have several different browsers on each machine, and several individuals might share the same computer...).

● It is possible for the user to delete the cookies on a browser from time to time (and more common among the more technically literate – or suspicious – audiences). This effectively destroys the unique user from the perspective of the web site, and creates a new one when the user next visits. Over time, this will inflate the number of unique users visiting the web site.

Perhaps all of these factors, some under-counting, some over-counting, will cancel each other out, leaving us with a fairly reliable idea of our user numbers. Or perhaps not. The fact remains that all of these unknowables, compounded together, make the assumption that tokens in cookies represent actual unique individuals highly contentious at best, and at worst, completely misleading.

In the face of such strong evidence against the use of cookies to represent identity, should anyone still be using them to track users? From the standpoint of the strict skeptical analyst, clearly not, but this is not the end of the story. In the next section, we will examine how the adoption of common standards for web traffic analysis is an attempt to overcome the problems detailed so far, and draw the boundaries inside which we can make some assumptions about our user behavior.

Standards for Web Traffic Analysis

We can see that this subject is fraught with confusion and competing claims, ideas, and definitions. Different methods for analyzing traffic give us different perspectives on user behavior, but disagreements persist as to what we can or cannot know. In the extreme case, should we even try to measure anything except the strain on our web server to cope with demand? Well, life is a complicated place and, as in other fields, there are ways of making sense of an apparently daunting and complex confusion of information. In this section we will look at the standards that are being developed to clarify the situation, and discuss what these standards are designed to achieve.

There is a movement to promote standards for web measurement lea by organizations with responsibility for auditing companies' circulation, originally in an offline advertising context, but increasingly in the digital arena. In particular, the International Federation of Audit Bureaux of Circulations (IFABC) has established a Web Measurement Committee, currently chaired by the UK, which has drawn up a set of standard definitions. The IFABC was founded in Sweden in 1996, and currently represents 36 Audit Bureaus in 32 countries.

We should now examine the standards recommended by this committee in a little detail. Once we have established the suggested terms and definitions, we can examine how and why these were chosen, what purpose they are designed to serve, and the extent to which they answer the objections of the skeptical analyst.

Metrics

The committee has a whole range of different metrics and measurements, many related to the auditing of advertising, and also to other digital areas, such as e-mail or WAP access, but the measurements that are most relevant to our discussion are summarized opposite.

- **Hits**
  This is a highly ambiguous term. Originally, "hits" referred to the number of files downloaded from the web server – equivalent to Analog's use of the term "requests". Over time, however, the use of the term has mutated, and many people seem to use it to mean what we would normally refer to as page views or impressions. Due to this ambiguity, the term "hits" is rejected as a standard measure.

- **Page Impression**
  This is sometimes referred to as "page view", though "impression" is adopted as the standard term. A page impression is a single file, or collection of related files, sent by the web server to the user as a result of a single request made by that user. The important point here is that only one page impression can be counted for each single user-initiated request. For example, if the user clicks on a link and requests a page, and that page contains several image files which the browser also requests from the server, then this counts as a single page impression. Images are not the only factor to filter out here (CSS files, for instance). The more obscure consequence of this definition concerns pages that include frames, which in turn display several (HTML) files. There is one page impression per user-initiated request, no matter what the type of file.

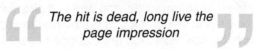

> *The hit is dead, long live the page impression*

- **Unique Host**
  A host is represented in the log file by the client computer's IP address. A unique host is therefore a unique IP address in the log.

- **Unique User**
  This is intended to identify an end user, as opposed to a host, which can in practice represent several unique users. The unique user is defined as a Cookie ID or token, or a registration ID, or a combination of client IP address and User agent (effectively the browser-Operating System combination)..

- **Single and Repeat Unique Users**

  A single unique user is a unique user that has only made one visit to the site, and a repeat unique user is one who has visited the site more than once. Both of these measures are expressed as a percentage of total unique users.

- **Visit**

  A visit is defined as a sequence of page impressions requested by a single unique user before a gap of 30 minutes between requests by that unique user. This is similar to a "user session".

- **Visit Duration**

  This is a calculation of the average length of a visit on the site, defined by the total amount of time for all visits of more than one page impression, divided by the total number of visits of more than one page impression. This is measured in seconds.

- **Unique Visit Duration**

  This is a calculation of the average total length of time that unique users spend on the site over a given period. It is defined by the total amount of time for all visits, divided by the total number of unique users for the given period, and again is measured in seconds.

Some of these standard measurements are clearly useful, and others appear more controversial. Rejecting the term "hits", for example, will come as a great relief to everyone, as the term has long since ceased to hold any real meaning, and yet its continued use has a degrading effect on attempts to conduct sensible web traffic analysis. Likewise, nailing down a definition of page impressions to replace what some people might previously have referred to as a hit is a positive move. The hit is dead, long live the page impression. Some other measurements, however, seem to break all of the rules established by the skeptical analyst.

Take the definition of unique users, for example. We have seen that using the IP address as a representation of actual individuals is highly misleading, hence the requirement to combine IP address with user agent. But is this enough? After all, combining one flawed measure with another flawed measure surely just produced a combined flawed measure of indeterminate value?

Imagine a typical user, behind a company firewall, and with Netscape and Internet Explorer on their PC. This user will still appear as two unique users to the web site, with one user agent/IP address combination for each browser. If cookies are used, this individual will still be double counted, as each browser would have its own cookie anyway. On the other hand, two different individuals in the same company are more likely to have the same user agent identity, as many corporations will have universal IT policies which co-ordinate the upgrade of their systems. If these two users do not accept cookies, they will appear as a single unique user to the web site.

Combining two uncertainties does not necessarily cancel out uncertainty, but rather compounds it. In practice, we would have no idea of the extent to which the over-counting/under-counting is resolving itself, and we cannot safely draw conclusions about actual numbers of unique users on this basis.

We have also discussed the dangers of calculating time spent on our web site by using the timings of requests, as the time spent on the final page is not accessible to us, at least by standard log file analysis techniques (some tagging solutions claim to record time spent on each page using JavaScript). Again what we see represented by these standard definitions is an attempt to analyze the unknowable. So, other than replacing hits with page impressions as a standard unit of measurement, are these definitions of any use at all? I think they are, but only if we know exactly what we are doing with them, and where the line between usability and confusion should be drawn.

It is important to understand what these organizations are trying to achieve by setting these standards, as this gives us an important guide to why and how the decisions were made. The standards are drawn up by organizations with experience of and responsibility for auditing circulation figures. So what is the purpose of auditing in this context? Fundamentally, the goal of the audit is to allow the companies, or third parties, to review the audited figures and make comparisons as a result. It is this principle of comparability that is at the heart of the standards that are being devised, and perhaps rightly so.

We have seen that it is extremely difficult, not to say impossible, to determine exact numbers in web traffic analysis. In attempting to set the standards, therefore, this is not the goal. The purpose of defining standards is essentially twofold:

- Firstly, to establish a common vocabulary, so that everyone can discuss the topic and understand what everyone else is talking about, remove misleading terms, and so on.

- Secondly, to establish auditable rules that will allow web sites and third parties to assume with a fair degree of confidence that they can compare one site's figures with another.

Once we reject the idea that audited web traffic measures tell us the absolute truth about a web site's world, and accept that they give us a way to talk sensibly about how one web site can be compared to another, then the standards defined above start to make more sense.

Take the example of the definition of a unique user, by combining the IP address with the user agent. Now in reality, this is not a measure of unique users, but it is still possible to compare the unique user number from site A with that of site B with some qualifications, if the measure was determined using the same criteria.

Two very different sites, let's say a news site and a toy retailer, might have difficulties in comparing figures, because the types of user accessing the site (including home users, children, workers in large corporations) are themselves very different. In other words, there is more uncertainty, and inaccuracies will most likely be exaggerated. In practice, however, we want to compare sites that are very alike, with similar demographic profiles, and so these inaccuracies will be reduced.

The same principle can be applied across the other measures being standardized. In the case of timings of visits, if we effectively ignore the time on that last page we reject the idea of "what really happened", and replace it with "what can we measure consistently across other similar sites", then the standards start to make more sense. In fact, the argument that scientists often reject "reality" in favor of "what can I measure" is one that has been debated by philosophers for a long time now, but that is perhaps another story.

Another advantage of the standards and definitions is that it provides a framework to be used once technology does allow us to count these things. In the first section we discussed the use of "tagging" to determine more accurate traffic data, and this includes the potential for calculating the time spent on the last page of the visit. By applying the standard definition to all sites that use this consistent method of determining visit times, we can arrive at more reliable and useful measures.

This last point illustrates an advantage, but also a crucial danger in the adoption of these standard definitions. Different measuring techniques will give different figures for the same standard measure on the same site. If we calculate our unique users by counting distinct IP/user agent combinations, and then recalculate it using cookie tokens, we will almost certainly produce two quite different totals (excepting a rather bizarre coincidence, or a site with a very small number of unique users). In effect, we have a single definition of each element, but several variants of that element, depending on the method used for producing the data.

The role of the auditor is crucial. The auditor will first of all verify that the raw data was collected in an acceptable way, and that the necessary exclusions have been made, removing robot traffic from page impressions, for example. Secondly they will check that the measures reliant on the standards (the skeptical analyst might refer to these as "assumptions") have been calculated correctly. And finally, the auditor must release the verified information in the right context. In other words, ensure that when we are comparing traffic numbers, we are genuinely comparing like with like: cookies with cookies, and tags with tags.

> *Applying standards and employing auditors is not a replacement for proper intelligent interrogation of the data that is being presented*

One final warning. The auditors are the referees in the process, they check that everyone has followed the rules, and they make decisions and clarifications. They make it possible for those of us who understand the rules, why they exist, and the extent of their limitations, to make educated judgments about the information as it is presented. The danger of well-audited traffic data is that there is a great temptation, albeit amongst those less well versed in the complexities of web traffic analysis, to read more into the numbers than is reasonable. Auditors diligently point out that measures arrived at through different means cannot be compared, but it is likely that many people casting a more casual eye over the audited figures might well miss this distinction. "An audited number is an audited number, is it not?" Well, no. It is a starting point for examination, not a conclusion.

While it would be just magnificent if everyone in the known universe working with web sites bought a copy of this book (and read it), we must assume that many of our co-workers will miss out. In a world in which it is difficult to stop people talking randomly about hits, how much more difficult will it be to convince people of the fine distinctions between user agents and cookie tokens when calculating unique users? Surely an audited figure is an audited figure, and we can happily compare one with another? For many, standards, definitions, and auditors are there to remove the "well, it depends" from the debate. Yet the important fine distinctions remain, and can make all the difference. This is why it is crucial that, while we may adopt the standards that are being proposed, and indeed benefit greatly from so doing, we do not forget the purpose for which they were devised, and the scope within which they can be usefully applied. Applying standards and employing auditors is not a replacement for proper intelligent interrogation of the data that is being presented.

Summary

The rules of web traffic analysis: We have found that the process of accurate data collection and interpretation is somewhat complex, and that standards go some way to ironing out the confusion, but also introduce potential misunderstandings of their own. The important point is at all times to be very aware of what it is that is being analyzed, where the data came from, and the ultimate purpose of the analysis.

The first rule of web traffic analysis is that any measure or metric produced is extremely context-sensitive. The adoption of standards allows us to compare apples with apples, and oranges with oranges, but make sure you are not carrying a sack full of bananas, as you will be sure to slip on some of them. In fact, this does not only apply to statistical measures, but to all elements of web site traffic analysis.

Web sites are constructed for any number of different reasons, and audiences. So not only do we have news sites and toy retailers, we also have auction sites, sites with information

> *the user should be at the center of any analysis*

aimed at the working professional, the professional at leisure, children, retired people, pet lovers, religious people, extreme sports enthusiasts, and women called Susan. Some sites are free of charge, others are subscription only, some are funded by advertisers, others by government agencies, and so on. All of the users of these sites have subtle (and sometimes not so subtle) differences in their expectations, needs, and tolerances.

The second rule of web traffic analysis, therefore, is that the user should be at the center of any analysis that is undertaken. As the owner or administrator of the web site, you know your business, and your customer, better than anyone else. If they want lots of personalization, and you need to track them in great detail in order to customize their options, then you know that. If you are providing an online financial services application in which confidentiality and discretion are the prime drivers of your business, then the moment you so much as wave a cookie in your customers' general direction, you might see your profits crumble into dust. And no level of intelligent tracking and analysis will bring them back.

In the second half of the book, we will take a detailed look at how three very different web sites handle the issue of customizing traffic analysis to the specific needs of the web site and its users. What they all have in common, however, is that they understand the nuances of the business that they are in, and this intelligence is at the heart of the analysis that they do.

Analytics Techniques

2

- Using your own system
- Deciding what to track
- Storing the data

Author: Peter Fletcher and Ben Pearce

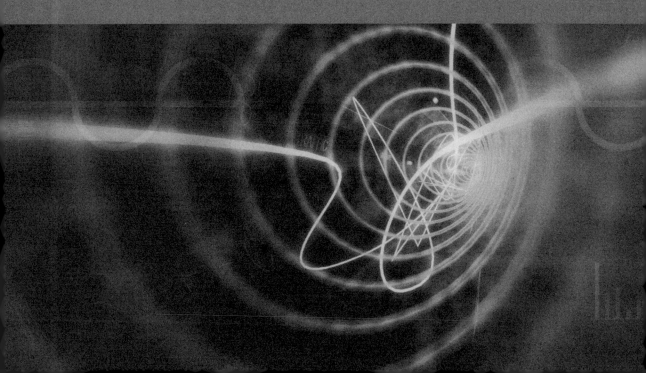

Database Log Analysis

In this chapter we will examine in detail a database log analysis implementation. There are two quite separate reasons for this. Firstly, it will give us a more intimate understanding of the data contained in a standard log file, and what can be achieved by importing it into a customized database to be mined for specific information. Secondly, by looking at the code being used, you will be in a position either to customize the database for your own purposes, or at least acquire a level of understanding of the principles involved in developing a new implementation using the tools and languages with which you are most familiar.

As we walk through the various coding elements, we will not only be examining the specific operation of each code example, but also the structural function that it performs. Therefore, although this implementation is developed principally using Microsoft Access with VBA, the general principles that it exemplifies can be applied to almost any database and coding solution.

The implementation gives us the following functions:

- Setting a UserID ("token") in a cookie on the user's browser (from an *.asp* page)
- Importing log data into the Access database
- Organizing the data in the database to suit our analysis requirements
- Running queries and producing reports on data in Access (and Excel)

Note that an empty copy of the database is available from *http://www.glasshaus.com* – you didn't think we were going to give you our hard-won log files, did you?

Dealing with the Token

The first stage in the process is to set a cookie token to track unique users of the site (see *Chapter 1* for more on the drawbacks to using cookies). There are various methods of setting cookies; in the case studies in this book we will see an example of a site that uses a custom (COM+) component, and one that uses an Apache module. In this example, however, we will see how easy it is to manage cookies with simple script in a file that is inserted at the top of all the pages on the site being monitored.

As it is essential that this script is on every page of the site, we have placed it in a file that is then added to every page by using the server-side include command in ASP. This will include cookie details, but also other useful functions and constants that are applicable to the whole of the site. The included file itself is kept in the *_private* directory, which IIS knows not to serve as a web page, but only to make it available to internal parts of the site, as in this example of a server-side include:

```
<!— —#include virtual="/_private/toppagecode.asp"— —>
```

The cookie setting code is in two logical sections: the first generates the random token, and the second handles the setting, or updating, of the cookie itself. The principle of the token is that it is different from all other tokens set by the site. The script below takes a very straightforward approach to this, by simply concatenating the date and time on the server with a large randomly generated string of numbers. This does not technically give us a guaranteed unique token: there is an extremely small chance that two visitors receiving their first cookie from this site in the same second will be allocated the same randomly generated number. There are more complicated ways of guaranteeing a unique number, for example by connecting to a database and collecting a primary key to include in the token. To simplify this example, however, we have adopted a more straightforward solution, which is nevertheless effective and efficient.

Token Creation

Let us now turn to the code itself. Declare the function and reset the ASP *Randomize* function, then declare two variables, one for the full token, and another for the random number:

```
function GenerateToken()

    Randomize

    dim strToken
    dim strRandom
```

Use the ASP *Rnd* function to create a random number with a value greater than or equal to zero and less than one, multiply this by a large number (one billion), and convert the result to a string:

```
strRandom = cstr(Rnd * 1000000000)
```

If there is a decimal point, remove it using the *Replace* function:

```
strRandom = Replace(strRandom, ".","")
```

Get the current date and time by calling the *Now* function, and convert the result to a string, then concatenate this with the random string, and set the result to be the value of the token variable. We have also used the *Replace* function to remove extraneous symbols in the date:

```
strToken = cstr(now) & strRandom
strToken = Replace(strToken, " ","")
strToken = Replace(strToken, "/","")
strToken = Replace(strToken, ":","")
```

Assign the resultant string to be the return value, and then end the function:

```
GenerateToken = strToken
```

```
end function
```

Now that we have a function that generates the token, we can use it as part of the cookie management script.

Cookie Management

First, declare the name of the cookie as a constant, as it will be used throughout the script, and also a variable to hold the value of the cookie token – if there is one – in the request.

```
const COOKIE_NAME = "Token"
```

```
dim strCookieToken
```

Now we employ the useful ASP *Cookies* collection to retrieve the value of the user's token, sent in the request. If the user has not visited the site previously, or has cookies disabled, the value of the token will be blank (in this context, a string of zero length):

```
strCookieToken = Request.Cookies(COOKIE_NAME)
```

Next, we check to see if the token has anything in it. If it is empty, then we send a new cookie in the response, using the GenerateToken function:

```
if len(strCookieToken) = 0 then
  Response.Cookies(COOKIE_NAME) = GenerateToken
```

Now we need to set the other properties of the cookie, namely the expiry date, set to three months from the current date, and the path. Setting the path to `"/"` means that the cookie can be accessed by code on pages in all directories of the site:

```
Response.Cookies(COOKIE_NAME).Expires = dateAdd("m", 3, now)
Response.Cookies(COOKIE_NAME).Path = "/"
```

Now we can set our cookie, we need to attend to the users who have returned a cookie in the request. Here we need to reset the expiry date to three months' time, and then also send the other properties of the cookie. This is very important, as the cookie we send in the response will overwrite the one the user already holds, so if we did not resend the other details – the token and the path – these would effectively be deleted on the user's machine:

```
else
  Response.Cookies(COOKIE_NAME) = strCookieGUID
  Response.Cookies(COOKIE_NAME).Expires = dateAdd("m", 3, now)
  Response.Cookies(COOKIE_NAME).Path = "/"
end if
```

As the GenerateToken function and the cookie setting code belong together, it makes sense to keep them in the same script. The full version of the code that is stored in the toppagecode.asp include file is as follows:

```
const COOKIE_NAME = "Token"

dim strCookieToken

strCookieToken = Request.Cookies(COOKIE_NAME)

if len(strCookieToken) = 0 then
  Response.Cookies(COOKIE_NAME) = GenerateToken
  Response.Cookies(COOKIE_NAME).Expires = dateAdd("m", 3, now)
  Response.Cookies(COOKIE_NAME).Path = "/"
else
  Response.Cookies(COOKIE_NAME) = strCookieToken
  Response.Cookies(COOKIE_NAME).Expires = dateAdd("m", 3, now)
```

```
    Response.Cookies(COOKIE_NAME).Path = "/"
end if

function GenerateToken()

  Randomize

  dim strToken
  dim strRandom

  strRandom = cstr(rnd * 1000000000)
  strRandom = Replace(strRandom, ".","")

  strToken = cstr(now) & strRandom
  strToken = Replace(strToken, " ","")
  strToken = Replace(strToken, "/","")
  strToken = Replace(strToken, ":","")

  GenerateToken = strToken

end function
```

Now that we have cookie tokens in the requests to the site, we can pick them up by ensuring the web server is set to record them in the *cs(cookie)* field in the log file. In the rest of this chapter we will look at how to turn these log files into valuable searchable information in an Access database.

The Database

One of the key facets of this database solution is the fine-grained ability for the analyst or administrator to specify exactly which data are required, and which are extraneous and can be filtered out. Because we are using a database, we can organize all data collected according to the requirements of the site, and construct queries to answer specific, and often very detailed, questions.

The database itself consists of two sets of tables: those containing the actual parsed log data, and those used by the analyst to configure the data according to the requirements of the analysis. We will go through the workings of the database in detail shortly, but first we can take an overview of the basic structure:

Admin Tables

`tblPages`	This contains the URIs of all the pages on the site that are to be counted when calculating page impressions. This gives the analyst a lot of control over what is and is not counted, and each page is also designated a Category in the `tblCategories` table.
`tblCategories`	The analyst can designate categories, such as "article", "site information page", "search", and so on, and these categories are referenced by `tblPages`.
`tblLinkIDs`	We track the click-throughs to the site by counting referring pages that contain a `LinkID` in the query string, and these Ids are generated by and sorted in `tblLinkIDs`. The analyst can add a new record to the table, which will generate a unique ID number, and this can be positioned in the query string of the new link to be used, in the form `linkid=000001`

Data Tables

`tblLogs`	This contains the parsed data from the log file. Individual queries can then selectively extract data from this table - referrers or cookies, for example - and place then in data tables of their own (detailed below). Once these tables have been updated, the contents of `tblLogs` are deleted, as this table will otherwise become full of data that will not be used.
`tblpageViews`	This contains details of the page views, where pages are defined in `tblPages` detailed above.
`tblCookies`	This contains the tokens from the `cs(Cookie)` filed in the logs, and a count of the number of times that token appeared for each date.
`tblReferrers`	This contains the full URI, including the query string, of the pages referring request to the site, and a count of the number of times that the URI appeared for each date
`tblLinkClickThroughs`	This contains the link Ids that referred requested to the site, and a count of the number of times that `linkID` appeared for each date.

To get a feel for how this works, we shall now look at the code that imports the log data into the database, which is contained in an Access module. This code essentially spells out the logic of the import process, and calls upon other queries to specify the details of the data to be imported. We can therefore review the module code first to give us an overview, and then delve a little deeper into the specifics of each subcomponent.

The Import Logs Module

First we set up the module, declare the function, and set the variables. We also turn off the automatic warnings, which prevents the import process being interrupted by dialog boxes warning us that we are about to write to the database:

```
Option Explicit

Function ProcessFile()
```

```
Dim intDataExists As Integer
Dim dtmDateOfFile As Date
Dim strFileDate As String
Dim strFileName As String
Dim strPath As String
Dim strReportName As String
Dim strFileNameLOG As String

'Turn off database warning messages
DoCmd.SetWarnings False
```

The function is called from an Access form, which requires the user to enter the date of the log file to be processed. Here the date is retrieved and the value stored in a variable:

```
dtmDateOfFile = Forms!frmRunImport!dtm_FormDate
```

We need to check that the data has not already been imported into the database. The module runs a query, which checks whether any data exists (in tblPageViews), and if so produces a warning message and exits the module:

```
intDataExists = Application.DMax("[CountofRecords]", "qryCheckForData")

If intDataExists >= 1 Then

    MsgBox "Data for this date already imported!"
    DoCmd.SetWarnings True

    Exit Function

End If
```

The function has been coded to assume a specific format for the log file name, based on the date. Obviously it is essential to ensure that the log files to be analyzed have their names set to the correct format. It then works out the file name by taking the date value captured above, specifying a specific format for the date, converting it to a string, and then adding the ".txt" suffix. The suffix is important so that Access understands that the format of the file to be imported is a plain text file. We also need to specify the path to the file, so that Access can find it:

```
strFileName = Format(dtmDateOfFile, "yymmdd")
strFileName = CStr(strFileName)
strFileName = strFileName & ".txt"
strPath = "C:\logfiles\"
```

For example, if we tell the database we want to process the logs for September 15th 2002, Access would look in the `c:\logfiles\` directory for a file with the name `020915.txt`.

Now we tell Access to find the specified file. First we give instructions as to where to find it (notice that this opens a `With` command):

```
With Application.FileSearch
          .NewSearch
          .LookIn = strPath
          .FileName = strFileName
          .MatchTextExactly = True
```

Then we execute the search, checking to see whether the search returns a file or not:

```
If .Execute() > 0 Then
```

If the search returns a result, then we begin to import the data. Using Access's `TransferText` command, specify that the format of the file is included in `spcLogFile`, which table to import the data into (`tblLogs`), and the path and filename of the log file to be imported:

```
DoCmd.TransferText acImportDelim, "spcLogFile", "tblLogs", [&_]
strPath & strFileName, False
```

Now we run the import queries in turn.

The Import Queries

> **!** Note the `acEdit` constant used here specifies that the query being run is editing existing data in a table, as apposed to adding new data – `acAdd` – in the previous queries

Each of these queries selects data from the `tblLogs` table, and appends it to data in a separate table in the database. This section is highly customizable, and new tables and queries can be added as appropriate. The queries that are included here relate to the cookies, page requests, referrers, and click-throughs from links on other sites, or in mail-outs.

```
DoCmd.OpenQuery "qryAppendCookies", , acAdd
DoCmd.OpenQuery "qryAppendPageViews", , acAdd
DoCmd.OpenQuery "qryAppendReferers", , acAdd
DoCmd.OpenQuery "qryAppendLinkClickThroughs", , acAdd
```

Once the data has been imported into the correct tables, the raw data in the `tblLogs` table can be discarded. This will save space and improve efficiency, but it is optional as – space permitting – it might be helpful to hold on to the raw data for future analysis.

```
DoCmd.OpenQuery "qryDeleteLogsContent", , acEdit
```

Clean up by closing the import form that runs the import module:

```
DoCmd.Close acForm, "frmRunImport", acSaveNo
```

Remembering that we are still in an If clause, we need to handle the case where, for whatever reason, the function did not find the file we specified. This code generates a message box specifying the date that has failed to produce a log file, and then, as above, closes the form, and then we can close the If clause.

```
Else

  MsgBox "Log File for " & dtmDateOfFile & " is not there!"
  DoCmd.Close acForm, "frmRunImport", acSaveNo

End If
```

Finally, clean up, by closing the With clause, and then turn the warnings system back on, and end the function:

```
End With

DoCmd.SetWarnings True

End Function
```

Now we can turn to the functions and queries referred to in the import module. The first one is the form that triggers the import process. The idea here is that the analyst can specify a date, and the import script will go find the file (or files, if the script is suitably amended) that relate(s) to that date, and process the data therein.

Starting the Import Process (frmRunImport)

Many of the queries that are run as part of the database analysis implementation are configurable to be accessed from a form. In the case of the Import Module, frmRunImport allows the analyst the opportunity to enter the date of the log file to be imported, and the module script has been programmed to accept this input and run. The form defaults to yesterday's date since that is the latest log file the system will have and will generally be the one most likely to be dealt with:

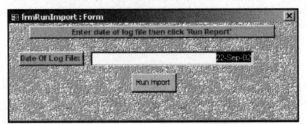

The form to run the import process from

Specifying the Format (spcLogFile)

Access features a handy tool to specify the format of the external data being imported, which we make use of. The idea is that this specification can be made once, then simply referred to in the module script, and Access will know how to parse the file. On this occasion, the data is being imported into tblLogs, for use by the Append queries, and so we have identified the fields in the log file that relate to the fields on tblLogs. These are:

- date
- c-ip
- cs-uri-stem
- cs-uri-query
- sc-status
- cs(User-Agent)
- cs(Cookie)
- cs(Referer)

To specify the format of a log file (or any other external data), go to *File > Get External Data > Import*. Then browse to a typical log file to bring up the Import Text Wizard. Click on the *Advanced* button, to bring up the *Import Specification* window, then enter the details of the log format required. We can skip fields that are in the log file but which we do not want to load into tblLogs. Once all the details are there, we can save the specification:

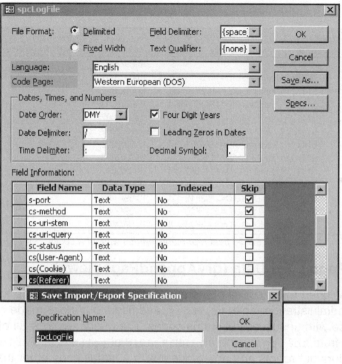

Saving an import/export specification

There are four `Append` queries in our module. These are essentially SQL scripts that `SELECT` data from the newly populated `tblLogs`, and `INSERT` it into the relevant table.

Adding the Cookie Data (qryAppendCookies)

This query produces a table with a summary of the cookie data from the log. It `SELECT`s the `Cookie` field and `Date`, and counts the number of instances of that cookie in `tblLogs` by counting the generic `Date` field instances. It then `GROUP`s the data by `Cookie` and `Date`, giving us a count of the number of instances of that particular `Cookie` for each date.

Here is the full query:

```
INSERT INTO
  tblCookies (Cookie, [Date], CountOfPageViews)
SELECT
  [tblLogs].[cs(Cookie)], [tblLogs].[date], Count([tblLogs].[date]) AS
CountOfdate
FROM
  tblLogs
GROUP BY
  [tblLogs].[cs(Cookie)], [tblLogs].[date];
```

And here is the table it produces:

RecordID	Cookie	Date	CountOfPageViews
814122	-	18/09/2002	857
814126	UserID=GUID=1%2F16%2F	18/09/2002	5
814127	UserID=GUID=1%2F16%2F	18/09/2002	5
814128	UserID=GUID=1%2F29%2F	18/09/2002	3
814129	UserID=GUID=1%2F3%2F:	18/09/2002	4
814130	UserID=GUID=1%2F31%2F	18/09/2002	1
814131	UserID=GUID=11%2F16%:	18/09/2002	5
814132	UserID=GUID=11%2F18%:	18/09/2002	3
814133	UserID=GUID=11%2F28%:	18/09/2002	2
814134	UserID=GUID=12%2F1%2F	18/09/2002	5
814135	UserID=GUID=2%2F12%2F	18/09/2002	8
814136	UserID=GUID=2%2F28%2F	18/09/2002	4
814137	UserID=GUID=3%2F23%2F	18/09/2002	1

tblCookies : Table

Note that the "-" field represents entries without a cookie.

Adding the Page View Data (qryAppendPageViews)

This query is designed to collect all of the successful requests for pages that are specified in an administration table, tblPages, and filters out those made by known robots, and those with unsuccessful status codes. The query SELECTs all of the requests for these pages from tblLogs using an INNER JOIN of tblLogs and tblPages. Then a WHERE clause filters out robots and any request with a status code other than 304, or one of the 200 series, which indicate a successful request. Naturally this is a highly configurable part of the process, and the SQL can be amended to include or exclude whatever you choose. Finally, the data is grouped by PageID and Date, producing a table (tblPageViews) detailing how many requests were successfully served for each page on each day.

The analyst needs to have specified in the tblPages table those pages that are of interest here:

CategoryID	Category
1	General Site Page
2	Article
3	Editorial
(AutoNumber)	

tblCategories : Table

The administrative table containing pages we want to track requests for

As an additional level of control, this table is also cross-referenced with another, tblCategories, so that each page can be designated as a type, allowing for detailed reports at a later stage.

Here is the full query:

PageI	Page	DatePutUp	Description	CategoryID
1	/Default.asp	25/05/2001	homepage	1
2	/about.asp	25/05/2001	about us	1
3	/archives.asp	25/05/2001	archive list	1
4	/contact.asp	25/05/2001	contact page	1
8	/editorial.asp	19/03/2002	editorial	3
9	/legal.txt	25/05/2001	terms and conditions	1
11	/register.asp	25/05/2001	email registration	1

The administrative table containing categories into which pages fit

```
INSERT INTO
tblPageViews ( PageID, [Date], PageViews )
SELECT
  tblPages.PageID, tblLogs.date, Count(tblLogs.date) AS CountOfdate
FROM
  tblLogs
INNER JOIN
  tblPages
ON
  tblLogs.[cs-uri-stem] = tblPages.Page
WHERE (
  tblLogs.[cs(User-Agent)] Not Like "*googlebot*"
AND
  tblLogs.[cs(User-Agent)] Not Like "*Infoseek*"
AND
  ([tblLogs].[sc-status] Like "2*" Or [tblLogs].[sc-status] = "304"))
GROUP BY
  tblPages.PageID, tblLogs.date;
```

Once run, the query produces a table containing a record of how many times each page in `tblPages` was requested each day:

RecordID	Date	PageID	PageViews
53696	18/09/2002	72	2
53695	18/09/2002	68	2
53694	18/09/2002	65	1
53693	18/09/2002	64	2
53692	18/09/2002	63	2
53701	18/09/2002	81	21
53717	18/09/2002	104	1
53654	18/09/2002	1	306
53724	18/09/2002	112	2
53723	18/09/2002	111	3
53722	18/09/2002	109	2
53721	18/09/2002	108	8

The resulting table showing views per page, by date

Adding the Referrer Data (qryAppendReferers)

This query collects all of the referring pages and counts them by date. Using the WHERE clause, we have opted on this occasion only to collect referrals to ".asp" or ".htm" pages (this is optional, and, of course, configurable to individual needs). The query then groups each referrer by date, and also filters out "internal" referrals:

```
INSERT INTO
    tblReferers (Referer, [Date], [Count])
SELECT
    [tblLogs].[cs(Referer)], [tblLogs].[date], Count([tblLogs].[date]) AS
CountOfdate
FROM
    tblLogs
WHERE (
    [tblLogs].[cs-uri-stem] Like "*.asp"
OR
    [tblLogs].[cs-uri-stem] Like "*.htm"
)
GROUP BY
    [tblLogs].[cs(Referer)], [tblLogs].[date]
HAVING
    tblLogs.[cs(Referer)] Not Like "*glasshaus.com*";
```

The resulting table looks like this:

	RecordID	Date	Referer	Count
▶	139915	18/09/2002	-	876
	139916	18/09/2002	http://aolsearch.aol.com/dirsearch.adp?query=soap%20interoperability	1
	139917	18/09/2002	http://ar.f133.mail.yahoo.com/ym/ar/ShowLetter?box=Inbox&login=1&uid=109	1
	139918	18/09/2002	http://associates.amazon.com/exec/panama/associates/join/developer/faq.ht	1
	139919	18/09/2002	http://associates.amazon.com/exec/panama/associates/join/developer/faq.ht	1
	139920	18/09/2002	http://associates.amazon.com/exec/panama/associates/join/developer/faq.ht	1
	139921	18/09/2002	http://associates.amazon.com/exec/panama/associates/join/developer/faq.ht	1
	139922	18/09/2002	http://associates.amazon.com/exec/panama/associates/join/developer/faq.ht	3
	139923	18/09/2002	http://au.dir.yahoo.com/computers_and_internet/internet/world_wide_web/We	1
	139924	18/09/2002	http://blackboard.bentley.edu/bin/common/msg_view.pl?pk1=28591&sos_id_	2
	139925	18/09/2002	http://ca.google.yahoo.com/bin/query_ca?p=%22intelligent+agents%22&y=o	1
	139926	18/09/2002	http://campusweb.vuntech.edu.tw/~course/cour/9114237.html	1

Referrers by site and date

Adding the Click-Through Data (qryAppendLinkClickThroughs)

This allows us to monitor specific links that we have created, for example in a marketing campaign, either in a mail-out, or links from a third-party site.

LinkID	Link	DateCreated	Description
1	mail1	23/08/2002	weekly mailout
2	mail2	30/08/2002	weekly mailout
3	mail3	06/09/2002	weekly mailout
4	asp1a	10/09/2002	asp campaign
5	mail4	13/09/2002	weekly mailout
6	asp1b	17/09/2002	asp campaign

The administrative table indicating links we want to track

The WHERE clause filters out all of the query strings which do not contain "linkid=", and from those remaining, selects the link id itself: the six characters immediately after this part of the string.

```
INSERT INTO
tblLinkClickThroughs ( [Date], FK_LinkID, ClickThroughs )
SELECT
tblLogs.date, Mid([cs-uri-query],InStr([cs-uri-query],"linkid=")+7,6) AS
ParseQS, Count(tblLogs.date) AS CountOfdate
FROM tblLogs
WHERE (
tblLogs.[cs-uri-query] Like "*linkid=*"
)
GROUP BY
tblLogs.date, Mid([cs-uri-query],InStr([cs-uri-query],"linkid=")+7,6);
```

The query produces a table much like this one:

RecordID	Date	FK_LinkID	ClickThroughs
6332	2002/09/18	21	3
6333	2002/09/18	1035	1
6334	2002/09/18	21	3
6335	2002/09/18	1035	1
6336		14	56
6337		14	654

Links clicked on by date

Clearing the tblLogs (qryDeleteLogsContent)

This one is rather straightforward, as it deletes all of the data from tblLogs, but keep the table itself, and its structure, ready for use next time the module code runs.

```
DELETE
  tblLogs.*
FROM
  tblLogs;
```

Once we have collected all the relevant data, and sorted it into the correct table structure, we can start to analyze the data by querying the database. This is an example of the sort of query that the data we have collected allows us to perform.

Finding Our Largest Referrer (qryRefererByDate)

The task is to find out who were our biggest referrers during a given period of time. To do this, we need to use the data collected in `tblReferers`, but then select each referrer by domain, and count the number of referrals generated. We start at the eighth character, as we can strip off the "`http://`" which we know is at the start of each referrer. Then we collect everything up to the first "/" character, giving us the domain name of the referrer. Then we specify the dates we are interested in using the WHERE clause, and finally group the data by the URI of the referrer, and order it most frequent first. The top row of the data produced by this query is blank, indicating that there was "no referrer". This would happen, for example, if the visitor had typed the URI straight into the browser, or clicked on a link from an email.

```
SELECT
   Left([Referer],InStr(8,[Referer],"/")) AS ReferrerURL,
Sum([tblReferers].[Count])AS SumOfCount
FROM
   tblReferers
WHERE (
   (tblReferers.Date>#9/17/2002#)
And
   (tblReferers.Date<#9/19/2002#)
   )
GROUP BY Left(Referer,InStr(8,Referer,"/"))
ORDER BY Sum(tblReferers.Count) DESC;
```

Again, the query produces results like these:

ReferrerURL	SumOfCount
	880
http://www.google.com/	164
http://google.yahoo.com/	13
http://www.theserverside.com/	12
http://www.google.ca/	8
http://associates.amazon.com/	7
http://technology.monster.com/	6
http://searchwebservices.techtarget.com/	6
http://www.google.de/	5
http://www.macromedia.com/	5
http://www.google.ch/	5
http://www.altavista.com/	4

Summary of referrers, by date

Page Views by Date

`qryPageViewsByCategory` simply selects all page views by date and by category:

```
SELECT tblPageViews.Date,
       tblPageViews.PageViews,
       tblPages.Page,
       tblCategories.Category
FROM
   (tblPages INNER JOIN tblPageViews ON tblPages.PageID =
tblPageViews.PageID)
      INNER JOIN tblCategories ON tblPages.CategoryID =
tblCategories.CategoryID;
```

This returns the data in a form that is not particularly helpful at first sight. This is where the built-in interactivity between Office applications can come in handy. Following is an example of how to return the above data into Excel, where it can be manipulated in several different ways to aid analysis and charting (of course, if you are not an Office user, there will be spreadsheet applications with similar functionality that you can use):

To allow Excel to communicate with the Access database, you first need to set up an ODBC system data source as follows:

First, open the *Data Sources* (ODBC) dialog box (*Control Panel > Administrative Tools*). Under the *User*, *System*, or *File* tab, click '*Add*' (*User* means the data source will be available to the user you are currently logged in under, *System* means it will be available to any user logged onto the machine you are using, *File* means you can save the data source file on a network for example, so that anyone can access it). Select M*icrosoft Access Driver (*.mdb)* then click '*Finish*'. Now type a relevant name for your data source and select your database:

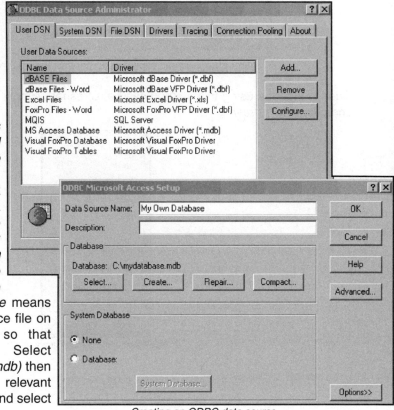

Creating an ODBC data source

Now, you can import the 'live' query directly into Excel as follows:

Within Excel, go to *Data > Get External Data > New Database Query...*
In the following dialog box you can then select your newly created data source. You will then be presented with the Microsoft Query Wizard where you can adjust the way the data will be transferred into Excel. Generally, as long as your query is set up correctly within Access, you can leave the settings as they are, and simply *Return Data to Microsoft Excel*.

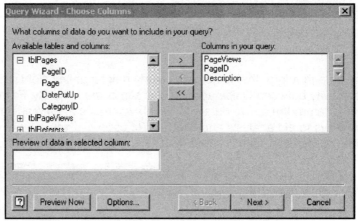

The query wizard allows us to choose the columns we want

Queries inserted using this method can be refreshed, simply by right clicking on them and choosing '*refresh*'

Refreshing data from the query

Once your data has been queried into Excel, you can use many of the powerful analysis features such as Pivot Tables to manipulate it to your liking. Below, `qryPageViewsByCategory` has been returned into Excel, and a Pivot Table has been run on it, summarizing the page views by category by date:

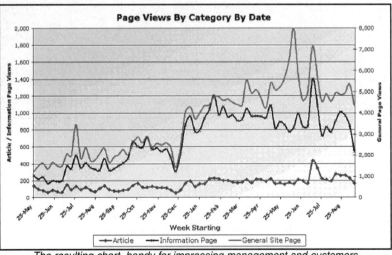

	A	B	C	D	E	F	G	H	I
1	Date	PageViews	Page	Category					
2	2001-05-25	54	/Default.asp	General Site Page					
3	2001-05-26	25	/Default.asp	General Site Page		Sum of PageViews	Category		
4	2001-05-27	20	/Default.asp	General Site Page		Date	Article	General Site Page	Information Page
5	2001-05-28	50	/Default.asp	General Site Page		2001-05-25 - 2001-05-31	136	1250	257
6	2001-05-29	444	/Default.asp	General Site Page		2001-06-01 - 2001-06-07	96	1499	217
7	2001-05-30	199	/Default.asp	General Site Page		2001-06-08 - 2001-06-14	84	1631	244
8	2001-05-31	458	/Default.asp	General Site Page		2001-06-15 - 2001-06-21	56	1344	163
9	2001-06-01	403	/Default.asp	General Site Page		2001-06-22 - 2001-06-28	85	1663	200
10	2001-06-02	85	/Default.asp	General Site Page		2001-06-29 - 2001-07-05	67	1498	191
11	2001-05-25	7	/20020915.asp	Article		2001-07-06 - 2001-07-12	63	1501	200
12	2001-05-27	2	/20020915.asp	Article		2001-07-13 - 2001-07-19	151	2070	375
13	2001-05-28	1	/20020915.asp	Article		2001-07-20 - 2001-07-26	92	1954	339
14	2001-05-29	62	/20020915.asp	Article		2001-07-27 - 2001-08-02	131	3462	502
15	2001-05-30	23	/20020915.asp	Article		2001-08-03 - 2001-08-09	90	1849	350
16	2001-05-31	41	/20020915.asp	Article		2001-08-10 - 2001-08-16	119	2348	407
17	2001-06-01	34	/20020915.asp	Article		2001-08-17 - 2001-08-23	86	1744	352
18	2001-06-02	5	/20020929.asp	Article		2001-08-24 - 2001-08-30	70	1772	334
19	2001-06-03	8	/20020929.asp	Article		2001-08-31 - 2001-09-06	105	2070	320
20	2001-06-04	11	/20020929.asp	Article		2001-09-07 - 2001-09-13	138	2337	460
21	2001-06-05	14	/20020929.asp	Article		2001-09-14 - 2001-09-20	94	1675	322
22	2001-06-06	19	/20020929.asp	Article		2001-09-21 - 2001-09-27	80	1919	340
23	2001-06-07	5	/20020929.asp	Article		2001-09-28 - 2001-10-04	73	2020	376
24	2001-06-08	4	/20020929.asp	Article		2001-10-05 - 2001-10-11	87	2271	408
25	2001-06-09	4	/20020929.asp	Article		2001-10-12 - 2001-10-18	92	2021	463
26	2001-06-10	5	/20020929.asp	Article		2001-10-19 - 2001-10-25	143	2520	658
27	2001-06-11	15	/20020929.asp	Article		2001-10-26 - 2001-11-01	167	2853	605
28	2001-06-12	25	/20020929.asp	Article		2001-11-02 - 2001-11-08	123	2589	594
29	2001-06-13	16	/20020929.asp	Article		2001-11-09 - 2001-11-15	123	2892	708
30	2001-06-14	15	/20020929.asp	Article		2001-11-16 - 2001-11-22	130	2377	572
31	2001-06-15	11	/20020929.asp	Article		2001-11-23 - 2001-11-29	116	2567	589
32	2001-06-16	2	/20020929.asp	Article		2001-11-30 - 2001-12-06	116	2492	545
33	2001-06-17	1	/20020929.asp	Article		2001-12-07 - 2001-12-13	111	2577	572
34	2001-06-18	6	/20020929.asp	Article		2001-12-14 - 2001-12-20	88	2381	471
35	2001-06-19	9	/20020929.asp	Article		2001-12-21 - 2001-12-27	51	1413	304
36	2001-06-20	11	/20020929.asp	Article		2001-12-28 - 2002-01-03	89	2321	520
37	2001-06-21	16	/20020929.asp	Article		2002-01-04 - 2002-01-10	163	4015	858
38	2001-06-22	10	/20020929.asp	Article		2002-01-11 - 2002-01-17	193	4293	962

Page views summarized by category by date

This data can then easily be charted using the built-in Pivot Chart functionality, or with your own customized one:

The resulting chart, handy for impressing management and customers

Unique Cookie Visitors by Day

This simple query just counts the unique cookies listed by day to tell you the number of different visitors with cookies enabled who visited the site (they are unique as in the query qryAppendCookies the aggregate function GROUP BY was used):

```
SELECT tblPageViews.Date,
       tblPageViews.PageID,
       tblPageViews.PageViews,
       tblPages.CategoryID
FROM tblPageViews INNER JOIN tblPages ON tblPageViews.PageID =
tblPages.PageID
WHERE (((tblPageViews.Date) Between [start date?] And [end date?]));
```

Total Clicks on a Particular Tracking Link

Finally, this example shows you how you can make further use of Access' forms to run queries. The form frmClicksOnTrackingLink allows the user to select from a list of all the tracking links created (by SELECTing from tblLinkClickThroughs) to find out how many clicks in total that link has had, as the command button runs this query:

```
SELECT tblLinkClickThroughs.Link,
sum(tblLinkClickThroughs.ClickThroughs)
FROM tblLinkClickThroughs
WHERE
((tblLinkClickThroughs.Link)=[Forms]![frmClicksOnTrackingLink]![cboTracki
ngLink])
GROUP BY tblLinkClickThroughs.Link;
```

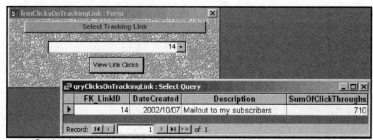

Seeing how many people clicked on a given link in a recent mail out

Summary

This chapter demonstrated how to process the data contained in log files. We set up a database to hold log file data and imported the logs into it, and then we looked at several different example queries. Although tools like Analog already process log file data, manipulating the data ourselves gives us the ability to do much more sophisticated data mining, gives us more flexibility in presentation, and allows us to fine-tune the analysis for very specific needs. It also gives us an opportunity to use tools like Excel to manipulate and present the data. The material covered in this chapter provides us with a basic framework that can easily be modified and tweaked to create a highly customized log file analysis application.

3

- **Legislation**
- **Guidelines and organizations**
- **Case studies from SmartGirl.org, The Onion, NYTimes.com**

Author: Peter Fletcher

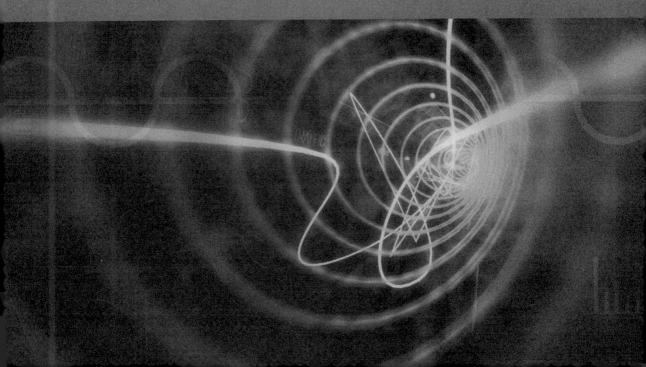

Privacy

So far we have been discussing the technical aspects of traffic analysis and data collection, but privacy is becoming a very important part of building and managing a modern web site. Now we review the main elements and concerns of the privacy issue, the legislative constraints that are being developed, and the various protocols, organizations, and programs that are trying to make privacy less daunting and problematic both for web professionals and users. We then put this in context, by looking at three case studies, which demonstrate how actual web sites are meeting the challenges that privacy presents to both the business of the Web, and user confidence. Finally, we wrap up with a summary of best practices and guidelines, suggesting the issues to cover in a privacy policy.

Concerns

Concerns over privacy can be categorized into several interlinked areas, which we will look at in turn. They are, briefly: the identification of individuals' behavior (often connected to the use of cookies), the collection and abuse of personal data (such as e-mail addresses), the security of the data once collected, and the ability to verify – and delete – incorrect data being stored.

Cookies

As use of the Web has grown, users have gradually become more aware of the fact that site owners can gather and store information about their movements through a site. A fear of the implications of this has been projected onto the main technical innovation that makes it possible: the cookie. Opinion about this humble text file varies from the entirely benign view that cookies do not identify individuals and can be disabled by the user, to the more extreme belief that they are a grave threat to our personal privacy, and should be avoided at all costs. What is the correct attitude towards the privacy implications of cookies?

> *There is no single "correct" attitude towards cookies, the situation changes depending on the circumstances*

There is no single "correct" attitude towards cookies, and, like much else that we discuss in this book, the situation changes depending on the circumstances: the type of site, the user, what is done with the cookie and the information that it generates, whether the cookie is "permanent" or deleted at the end of the browser session, and the ability of the user to opt out of any data collection. The basic fact of the cookie, however, is that it does not by default identify a known individual to the web site; it is merely an anonymous token that can be used to help the site deliver personalized pages to the user, or count the number of unique users (as defined in *Chapter 1*) that are visiting the site. This is complemented by the fact that users can disable cookies if they so desire, thus destroying any ability on the part of the site to track them, for whatever purpose.

Cookies are often used to identify an individual if the site that is using them requires some form of registration, either during a session in which the user has logged in, or from one session to the next, removing the obligation from the user to sign in each time on the same machine. For example, The New York Times on the Web (*http://www.nytimes.com/*) uses cookies to identify you between visits:

Before registering, the site doesn't know who we are

After we've registered and asked the site to remember us, it knows who we are next time we visit – in fact it welcomes us at the right-hand side of the header.

If we disable cookies before registering, or remove the cookies after registering, *NYTimes.com* no longer recognizes us.

Though we have established that cookies are not innately dangerous, there is a lot of uncertainty in the browsing public, and not all of it due to paranoia or misinformation, about how cookies work and what they can or cannot reveal. Concerns were raised, for example, when ad-serving company DoubleClick™ purchased Abacus Direct, a large catalog database firm. It was believed by some that this would allow DoubleClick to cross-reference its cookie data with the profiling information contained in the Abacus database. For more information on this case, we suggest that you visit the Electronic Privacy Information Center (*http://www.epic.org/*) and DoubleClick (*http://www.doubleclick.net/*).

Third-Party Cookies

These concerns came about because of third-party ad-servers' ability to place cookies on users' machines as they browse different sites. As we know from *Chapter 1* a cookie may only be retrieved by the server it was set by, which prevents any given web site from tracking the path of an individual user across the Web. Users visiting sites that use third-party ad-serving technology, however, might also receive a cookie from that server. This cookie is commonly referred to as a "Third-Party Cookie", as it is set not by the site the user is explicitly visiting, but by a completely different server. This same third-party server therefore technically has the ability to track its cookies as each individual user visits sites that use that ad-server, potentially building up a "profile" (albeit an anonymous one) of that user's surfing habits. This profile can be used to target ads at a user based on their surfing habits. Opinion is divided on this, as some feel this is a genuine benefit to the user, increasing the relevance of the information being served, while others consider it an intrusion into their private business. The key here, perhaps, is choice. DoubleClick, a provider of third-party ad-serving solutions, has introduced an "opt-out" cookie system, details of which are contained in their privacy policy: *http://www.doubleclick.com/us/corporate/privacy/privacy/default.asp.* Specifically, the policy states **"DoubleClick does not use your name, address, e-mail address, or phone number to deliver Internet ads. DoubleClick does use information about your browser and Web surfing to determine which ads to show your browser".**

Cookies have been designed to work in such a way that they do not of themselves pose a threat to privacy, but it is possible to deploy them in ways with which many users might feel uncomfortable. For this reason, it is important to be explicit in your privacy policy about exactly what cookies you set, and what you intend to do with the data collected as a result. We will cover this in more detail later in this chapter.

Data Privacy

The other broad area of concern for privacy is the collection, and integrity, of personal or sensitive information: this might include e-mail addresses, residential addresses, credit card details, purchasing history, medical information, and so on. The potential danger here is not that sites will be collecting information without the consent of the user, as it is fairly clear what is going on when a web site asks us to enter our address, but rather what happens to the data once we have clicked "submit ".

The factors that we need to consider are:

- What will the web site do with my personal information?
- How can I be sure that the web site will not use this information for purposes other than that to which I have consented?
- Will the web site intentionally distribute my personal information?
- Will the web site keep my information secure, and take steps to ensure that it is not unintentionally distributed?

As before, these are all key points that should be covered in any privacy policy, but there are also third-party agencies that can help us to gain the trust of our users, and these are also the main concerns of the various legislative bodies that have intervened in the interests of citizens' privacy. We will discuss some of the organizations that exist shortly, but first we're going to examine the more formal legislative controls that have been introduced.

Legislation

This section is intended to give a helpful overview of the legal constraints that are being introduced, concentrating on the situation in the US and the EU, with some suggestions for further research. Privacy legislation, like most legislation, is legally complex and technical, and circumstances will change between businesses and jurisdictions. Clearly, when considering your site's privacy policy and its terms and conditions, you should consider taking formal legal advice.

In this overview, we will consider the implications and intentions of two key legal interventions: the EU Data Protection Directive, and the US Children's Online Privacy Protection Act (COPPA). For details of the EU legislation, visit: *http://europa.eu.int/comm/internal_market/en/dataprot/index.htm*; and for more details on COPPA visit: *http://www.ftc.gov/bcp/conline/pubs/buspubs/coppa.htm*.

The EU Directive and "Safe Harbor"

The EU Directive binds all 15 member-states of the EU to safeguard the privacy of their citizens according to a basic set of principles, the intention being to harmonize and standardize the level of data protection and privacy across all of the member states. In principle, the legislation is designed to assert the following conditions:

- It covers those who collect, hold, or transmit personal data
- It puts them under an obligation to collect data only for "specified, explicit, and legitimate purposes"

- It obliges them to only hold data that is "relevant, accurate, and up-to-date"

- It mandates that the collection and retention of the data should be transparent, meaning it should be clear that the data collection and storage is being conducted, and that the individual has the clear right to opt out of this process

In particular, the Directive asserts the rights:

- To access the data being held

- To know where that data originated

- To rectify inaccurate data

- To legal recourse in the event of illegal use of the data

- To withhold permission to use the data for specific purposes (for example, sending spam or junk mail)

Furthermore, in the case of sensitive information, defined as "ethnic or racial origin, political or religious beliefs, trade union membership or data concerning health or sexual life", this can only be processed with the explicit consent of the individual (they have to OPT IN to this process).

There are various exceptions and provisos which refer to the rights and conditions, allowing a certain degree of flexibility in the drafting of this legislation by member states (for example, for legitimate "journalistic, artistic, or literary purposes"), and safeguards are required to be put in place to monitor this process. This flexibility is overseen by independent "data supervisory authorities" in each member state.

> The EU Directive is a formal guideline of principles for member-states to implement. Each state is free to draft legislation covering the Directive in its own manner, so long as it conforms to the Directive.

The impact of this legislation is that organizations (or, indeed, individuals) are not entitled to collect or process data about citizens of the EU without constraint. Data collectors must make clear what information is being collected, for what purpose, and provide the means for individuals to check the accuracy of the data held (and correct it if necessary), and opt out of certain uses of the data.

Whilst legislation within member-states specifically covers the use of data within the EU, and also the transfer of data between member-states, there is an assumption that EU citizens ought to be able to enjoy the same privacy and data protection rights regardless of the geographical destination of the data they provide. This therefore has an impact not only on web sites that operate from within the EU, but any web site that technically "transfers data" from inside of the EU zone. In effect, any web site hosted outside of this area is transferring data when it receives a request from an EU resident.

In order to avoid the potential for disputes between US companies and the EU, the US Department of Commerce and the European Commission created the Safe Harbor privacy framework, whereby US companies can verify that they will treat data collected from within the EU zone according to the standards outlined in the EU Directive. US companies can certify that they conform to the principles of the Directive, though the process is entirely voluntary, and can be undertaken either by joining a self-regulatory program (we look at one in the next section), or by developing their own program that conforms to the Safe Harbor framework.

The advantages to an organization conforming to the Safe Harbor framework are chiefly that they will accordingly be able to continue to do business with EU citizens and companies without interruption, and that any claims brought by EU citizens against US companies will, in most cases, be heard in the US. More information on the Safe Harbor framework can be found at the US Department of Commerce web site: *http://www.export.gov/safeharbor/*.

COPPA

The other significant piece of US legislation that we need to cover is the Children's Online Privacy Protection Act, known as COPPA. This Act sets out the legal framework for the collection of "personal information" from children under the age of 13. It applies to all web sites or "online services" that are aimed at children under 13 and that gather personal information from their users, and also to general web sites that have "actual knowledge" that they are collecting personal information from children.

The clear aim of this legislation is to safeguard the privacy of young children who may not be aware of the potential dangers of disclosing personal information over the Internet.

The clear aim of this legislation is to safeguard the privacy of young children who may not be aware of the potential dangers of disclosing personal information over the Internet. The Act covers information that individually identifies the child, such as name, address, e-mail, telephone, or anything that would allow someone to contact the individual. It also includes information such as hobbies and, importantly, information gathered by the use of cookies or other tracking devices "when they are tied to individually identifiable information" – that is, the cross-referencing of cookie data, such as pages visited by an individual, with that individual's contact information.

The Act places various constraints on the web sites to which it applies, the principal one being that the site must publish a clear and unambiguous privacy policy, and this should have a "prominent" link on both the home page of the site and any other page where personal information is collected. The Act specifies that the policy should state:

- Who is collecting the data – including the name, address, and e-mail address of at least one contact, and the names of any other parties ("operators") involved with the collection of data on the site

- What data is collected and how – included the use of cookies if appropriate

- Specifically what this information will be used for (direct marketing, sending an opt-in newsletter, etc.)

- Whether the information will be distributed to third parties, and if so for what purpose and with what safeguards. Also, parents must have the right to opt out of this third-party distribution of their child's information

- That no unnecessary information may be collected for the purposes of participation in the activities of the web site

- The parent's right to view, and if necessary remove, their child's personal information, and remove consent for further collection, as well as clear instructions as to how to carry this out

There are also a number of suitable definitions, clarifications, and exceptions to these rules, for example detailing what can be collected without the explicit consent of a parent. Nevertheless, the basic thrust of the Act is clear: when dealing with young children, the responsibilities of the web site for privacy and data protection are heightened, and explicit care must be taken to outline what is collected, why, and how the child or parent can intervene in the process.

Other Organizations

As the whole landscape of privacy, data protection, and legislation is complicated enough for web professionals, it is especially important to engender trust in the mind of the user. To this end, there are various organizations whose aim is to increase this sense of trust, and work with partner web sites to bring it about. Two such groups are BBBOnline (*http://www.bbbonline.org/*), run by the Council of Better Business Bureaus, and TRUSTe (*http://www.truste.org/*), an independent non-profit organization founded by the Electronic Frontier Foundation (EFF) and the CommerceNet Consortium. Both of these organizations have similar objectives and programs.

The general reason for the existence of organizations like BBBOnline and TRUSTe is to generate a greater sense of trust in Internet users, and the explicit policies that they advocate are broadly in line with the principles of the legislation that we have examined above. In short, users have the right to know what is being collected about them, what will be done with this information, including whether it will be further distributed, and the right to opt out of certain uses of the data, for example for direct marketing campaigns. The key to this is transparency: a privacy policy that states exactly what is being done, and what the user can do about it.

> *users have the right to know what is being collected about them*

With this objective of establishing clear and authoritative privacy policies, both of these organizations offer "Seal Programs", effectively underwriting the privacy policies of affiliated sites, and offering their "Seal" to indicate this. Whilst the details of how to join these programs vary, the basic principle is that the web site submits its privacy policy and data collection practices for review by the program. If the site meets the requirements of the program, both in terms of the policy itself and its general data practices, then it can be awarded the Seal (there is a fee for this service).

These programs also undertake to arbitrate in the case of any visitor entering into a dispute with the web site in question, and the site can be suspended or expelled from the program if it fails to live up to its promises, a facility designed to increase the level of trust and confidence in the web site's users. In addition to the main Privacy Seal Program, BBBOnline and TRUSTe also offer other programs, validating such things as children's privacy, and Safe Harbor compliance.

The Platform for Privacy Preferences Project (P3P)

A further attempt to clarify and simplify privacy for both web site operators and users has been made by the W3C in the form of the Platform for Privacy Preferences Project, commonly known as P3P. In essence, this is a project to standardize the information contained within privacy policies, and to encapsulate that information in a **machine-readable form**. The idea behind this is that if privacy policies can be made available in such a way as to be understandable to the user's computer, then this removes from the user the task of reading and interpreting the written version, effectively automating the task, once the initial preferences have been set. The idea is that this would make it far more likely that web sites' policies will be reviewed each time data is transferred.

This is an emerging standard for the construction of privacy policies, and with the credible backing of the W3C, so it is worth examining in a little more detail. Let's now take a brief look at how P3P works, what the web site operators and users need to do to use it, and discuss what effect this will, and will not, have on online privacy. There is some built-in support for P3P in Internet Explorer 6, Netscape 7, and as an additional feature for Mozilla (see *http://www.mozilla.org/projects/p3p/* and *http://lxr.mozilla.org/mozilla/source/extensions/p3p/*). Internet Explorer 6 now has a *Privacy* tab on the *Internet Options* dialog, allowing a simple selection of privacy preferences:

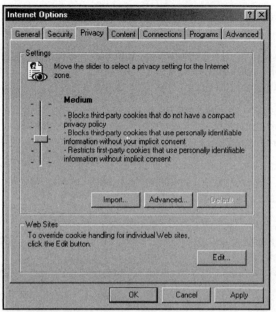

IE6 now lets you select your privacy preferences

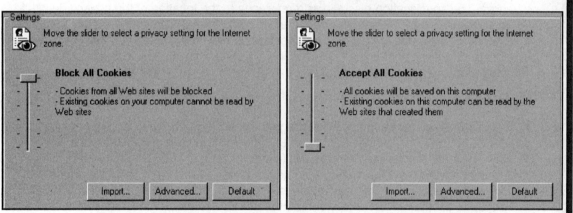

They range from total privacy (block all cookies) to none at all (accept all cookies)

P3P is a protocol for computers to exchange detailed information about privacy policies, in effect a language for discussing privacy. Specifically it defines a way in which a normal "natural language" privacy policy can be translated into an XML format, which user agents – browsers in most cases – can access, and check against a pre-defined set of preferences. A typical sequence of events is as follows:

1 A web site operator establishes what their privacy policy is, and writes a natural language version of it for display on the site.

2   The operator then translates this into an XML file using the P3P standard. There are various tools being developed to make this process easier.

3   Another XML file which contains details of where to find the policy is then placed in a "well-known location", which the W3C recommends is `/w3c/p3p.xml`, where the `w3c` directory is under the root of the site.

4   A user agent with P3P preferences set visits the web site, locates the privacy description and automatically downloads it, parses the contents, and compares it with the user preferences.

5   Based on this comparison, the browser can automatically elect to exchange data (a cookie, for example), with the web site, or warn the user that the site does not meet the standards specified in the preferences file in some way.

IBM is developing a P3P Editing tool, currently in beta, to ease the process of translating a written privacy policy into a machine-readable format (XML file). At the time of writing, this tool is free to download and use, and is available at: *http://www.alphaworks.ibm.com/tech/p3peditor*. A list of other implementations is available from the W3C web site: *http://www.w3.org/P3P/implementations*.

The location details do not necessarily have to be placed on the web site as detailed above. The specification also allows a reference to the location of the privacy details to be placed in the HTTP headers from the site, or in the HTML using a `<link>` tag. The process outlined above, however, represents the W3C's expectation of how most web site operators will deploy the reference in `/w3c/p3p.xml`, as this is probably the most straightforward and transparent method.

APPEL

The W3C are also working on a language for describing user privacy preferences, called APPEL (A P3P Preferences Exchange Language). The idea of **APPEL** is that it will be used to create sets of preference rules (called rulesets), which can then be imported into the browser (say) for making automated decisions regarding the exchange of data with web sites or other remote machines. The W3C do not expect individuals to learn APPEL to set their preferences, but rather use tools or ready-made rulesets to make the process easier. Existing rulesets, most likely created by a third party, can be imported into a browser, and indeed exchanged between different browsers operated by the user.

So now it seems we have at least an emerging standard for describing our privacy policy and automating the process of checking it. What is this designed to achieve? The wider adoption and implementation of P3P should:

- Make privacy policies more accountable. If browsers are automatically checking the details of a web site's policy, and acting accordingly on the preset user preferences, this will not only force sites to declare their policies unambiguously, but also ensure that the policies themselves are in line with their users' expectations. The principle is that privacy will become a more transparent process, meaning that users will be able to see clearly where they stand, and make informed decisions as a result.

- Enable users to have more control over their privacy and use of their personal information. It is unlikely that users currently check privacy policies in any detail (if at all) when visiting a site or exchanging data, largely due to the time needed to locate the policy and check it for potential problems. Automating the system, so long as the preferences-setting part of the process is clear, should increase awareness and control.

It is important to make clear, though, what P3P cannot do:

- It has no power to ensure that web sites actually abide by the privacy policy that they publish. There is nothing in the W3C specification that prevents a site from using P3P in an attempt to deceive their visitors. It could be argued that, as the system is automated, this may increase the potential for abuse, because users will begin to "trust" the browser to tell them when something is wrong. In fact, they should be trusting the web site, not P3P. In this respect, nothing has changed, as a site has always had the power to publish a misleading, or indeed false, privacy policy. This is where organizations such as TRUSTe or BBBOnline can be useful, and in fact P3P does contain a DISPUTE element in which dispute-resolution information can be described.

- P3P is not designed to supersede or replace statutory regulations, but rather complement them. The intention is that P3P will assist in the assertion of legal frameworks, and encourage a better understanding and conformity with them, but it cannot enforce them. Proper regulation and P3P go hand in hand.

- There is no provision for encryption or the security of data within the P3P specification. P3P does not replace the need for encryption and secure data exchange, but again complements it, by allowing the user to get a clear picture of what is being done, and to respond accordingly.

In summary, P3P is an important development in the privacy landscape. It has the authority of the W3C behind it, and has the support of many leading industry groups and companies. The adoption of P3P at the moment is somewhat nascent, but as newer browsers include elements of the specification in their upgrades, more users will become aware and able to take advantage of its preference checking process. In this respect, it will place the onus on web site operators – owners, managers, and developers – to create a clear privacy policy and implement it in P3P.

Case Studies: Real Life Privacy

We have so far covered something of the theory and the rules concerning online privacy, but the picture would not be complete without taking a look at how real sites are reacting to the situation. In this section we will discuss three different sites: *The Onion*, The New York Times, and *SmartGirl*. We will look at each site in turn, examining what it needs to do to maintain its business, what analysis is done, and how it explains this in its privacy policy. The information presented here is taken from interviews conducted with the help of the sites in question.

SmartGirl: www.SmartGirl.org

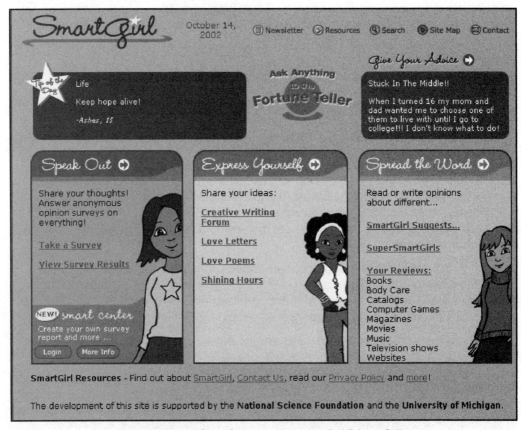

The front page of SmartGirl.org, with easy to find Privacy Policy

SmartGirl.org is a web site written for and by girls, many under 13 years of age, and therefore has to comply with COPPA. It is worth looking at how their exemplary privacy statement details what the site does and does not record, and the measures in place both to ensure compliance with the law, and create a safe and interesting place for girls to participate.

The policy begins with a statement of the site's purpose:

This site is owned by the University of Michigan and is operated by the Institute for Research on Women and Gender. Our mission is to create a place on the Internet where girls can feel free and safe to express their opinions and views on everything from the latest movies and the hottest fashion trends to everyday issues like school, relationships and navigating adolescence. Girls visiting the site can fill out reviews on different products (such as books, movies and CDs), take anonymous surveys, play games, or submit love poems, love letters, and other content to be posted on the site. Girls who become members can participate in the SmartCenter.

It ends by disclosing the name and address of the site's operators, with both postal and e-mail addresses for contact in the event of any queries. In between, there is a very explicit description of SmartGirl's privacy procedures.

Personal Information

This is defined as any information that can personally identify an individual, such as an e-mail address. The policy states that no visitor to the site is required to disclose such information for the purposes of participating in the site, and any e-mail address provided is done so entirely voluntarily. Specifically, *SmartGirl.org* will never post, publish, rent, sell, or intentionally distribute personally identifiable information. All work submitted, or survey completed, is anonymous – users can include an e-mail address for the purposes of receiving notification as to whether their work will be published, but once used this e-mail address is no longer linked to the individual user.

If the user is under 13 years of age, then their parent's consent is also required for their submission of an e-mail address, for example to join the newsletter, or to receive notification if they have submitted work. This is requested at the same time, and a message is sent to the parent, which is then used to notify the parent that the child's e-mail address has been received, and give them the opportunity to remove it.

WANT IN?
If you would like to subscribe, please enter your email address here and click "submit." If you are under 13, you must enter your parent's email address ALSO, because there is a US law that says we have to send them a note telling them you are getting the newsletter. SmartGirl NEVER shares your email address or your parent's email address with anyone, and will only use it to send you the newsletter. We throw your parent's email address away after we tell them you signed up for the newsletter. See our privacy policy for more information.

Your email address: _____

If you are under 13, we need your parent's email also: _____

[Submit]   [Clear all]

A parental e-mail address is required for girls under 13 to subscribe to the SmartGirl.org newsletter.

Parents can review their child's postings to the site, and change or delete their child's e-mail address or membership at any time. The privacy statement outlines the simple procedure for doing this.

User Tracking and Cookies

SmartGirl.org uses cookies for the following purposes:

- To track – anonymously – the traffic patterns on the site.
- To eliminate duplicate survey submissions.
- To allow members access to members-only content.

Crucially, cookies used for one purpose are not linked to cookies used for another purpose. For example, separate cookies are used for verifying survey submissions and traffic pattern analysis, and the two cookies are not identifiable as belonging to the same user. It is not possible to identify an individual user from the cookies stored on their computer. Other information, supplied by the web hosting company, is equally anonymous, and, similarly, released to third parties (such as advertisers) in aggregate form only. This information includes:

- Browser type and operating system (User-Agent)
- Sites referring users to *SmartGirl.org*
- IP address and Internet domains from which users are accessing the site
- Dates and times of distribution of traffic to the site
- Average length of stay on the site
- Pages visited

Opting In, Opting Out

As is implied above, the e-mail newsletter is strictly an opt-in list. Users voluntarily submit their e-mail address to be included on the newsletter and, in the event of the user being under 13 years of age, *SmartGirl.org* informs their parent of this, in case they wish to remove their child from the list.

Additional Measures and Security

In addition to the procedures detailed above, the site has strict policies regarding the security of the data collected:

Our Users' privacy and any personal information we may have about them are kept as secure as we are able, although like every other business entity, we cannot guarantee that this information will not be stolen. Passwords to access data at *SmartGirl* are only given to those trained to handle them safely. All *SmartGirl* staff members have signed confidentiality agreements that legally obligate them not to release e-mail addresses or any other information about visitors.

No personal information submitted by users is used for any purpose other than the stated reason for collection: e-mail addresses collected for the newsletter are used only to send the newsletter, and not for targeted mailings, for example. Furthermore, no personally identifiable information is ever distributed outside of the Institute for Research on Women and Gender Studies.

> *e-mail addresses collected for the newsletter are used only to send the newsletter, and not for targeted mailings*

The Onion: www.theonion.com

The well-known satirical news site.

The *Onion* is in the publishing business, which means that it makes its money by selling the print edition of the paper, and the advertising space therein. This is supplemented by its online business, which includes advertising sales, personals, and *The Onion store*, selling branded merchandising and other suitable wares. The online activity is important not only as a revenue stream in its own right, but also as a highly successful branding tool for the print publication. *The Onion* is aimed at an adult audience, with a notice declaring that it is not intended for readers under 18 years of age. Even though its content is irreverent and humorous, it takes online privacy very seriously.

Personal Information

The Onion collects and records personal information from customers, but only in order to fulfill orders that are made. This information includes the customer name, address, phone, e-mail (for order confirmation), and billing address if it is different from the shipping address. Credit card numbers are not stored by *The Onion*, but transferred to the card verification agent, *authorize.com*, who processes the order and confirms the result. If the transaction succeeded then the fulfillment details are forwarded to the fulfillment company for shipping. Users are able to register in order to speed up future interaction with the store, though this is entirely optional. Registration does, however, give the user the opportunity to review and amend any personal data that is stored about them on the site.

The Onion | Gambling-Addiction Study Gets Out Of Hand

Email This Page
Asterisk (*) indicates a required field.

* Your Name:

* Your Email:

* Friend's Name:

* Friend's Email:

Friend's Name:

Friend's Email:

Friend's Name:

Friend's Email:

Message:

NOTE: If emailing multiple people, the same message will be sent to each person.

Send This Page

Contact Us   Help/FAQ   Privacy Policy

The Onion® is not intended for readers under 18 years of age.

The only other collection of personal information on the site is the logging of e-mail addresses for the "E-mail this Story" feature. This is done as a security feature to protect *The Onion* from spam allegations. This information is not used in any other way.

Currently *The Onion* does not provide advertisers with demographic information gleaned from their campaigns on the site. Prior to a campaign, however, they are supplied with demographic data gathered from third-party sources (@plan, Nielsen) to help show potential clients the value of advertising with *The Onion*.

User Tracking and Cookies

Cookies are used on *The Onion* to maintain state during individual sessions. The information that this generates is then used to monitor visits to the site, though as the cookies are temporary – they expire at the end of the session – return visits by unique individuals are not tracked. An ad-tracking system – AdJuggler – is used to monitor general user responses to the ad campaigns on the site, in the form of ad impressions and click-throughs, but more detailed user interaction data is not recorded. The main purpose of the cookies used in advertising is to determine the frequency of the ads, and they use the cookie to control this for each unique visitor.

> *The main purpose of the cookies used in advertising is to determine the frequency of the ads...*

Cookies are also used for maintaining state as a customer moves through the shopping cart process. This cookie uses a unique anonymous user ID to keep each user distinct from others; the only data stored here is the expiration date and the name of the cookie, and no personal information is stored in these cookies. Each cookie is set using the ad system, or a piece of JavaScript embedded on each page.

> *...no personal information is stored in these cookies*

Data Analysis

The *Onion* outsources its log analysis to **I/Pro**, which gathers the information from the logs and sends it back in reports. I/Pro stores its extracted data in a database, but the final format can be `.xls` or `.csv` files, or a proprietary format for I/Pro Netline users. In addition to this, Analog is also used within the development team to generate more precise reports, for example, gathering browser version and OS data (from the User-Agent field). The I/Pro analysis is primarily to track page impressions, visits, and visiting organizations, resolved from the client IP address.

3

Privacy

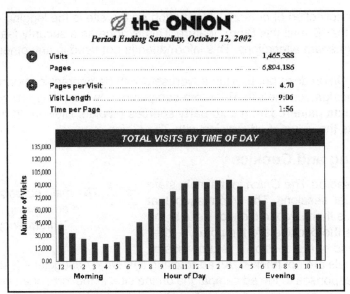

A typical day of visits at The Onion

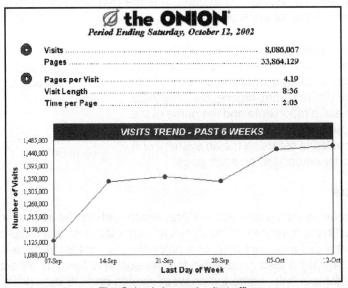

The Onion is increasing its traffic

This log analysis is not formally audited by an outside organization (such as ABC Interactive), but I/Pro implements the standards as part of their service, for example by filtering out robot traffic and "false" impressions. They say: "We have a rigorous IP exclusions list that removes most known spiders and robots. This list is maintained and updated on a regular basis. With the new Netline release, we will also be excluding spiders and robots based on the User Agent in [*The Onion's*] logs."

Opting In, Opting Out

The Onion does not currently operate any lists that would require an opt-out, however if they were to operate such lists they would favor a "double opt-in" approach. On occasion, advertisers have used contest pages to entice consumers to sign up for e-mail lists. These are opt-in lists for the third party, and this fact is specifically spelled out on these pages with a link to the advertisers' privacy policy. Sometimes this information is collected by *The Onion*, and then delivered to the advertiser at the end of the campaign, but no e-mail from *The Onion* is ever sent to people who choose to sign up for these contests.

Double Opt-in

A single opt-in typically occurs when a user joins a mailing list by giving their e-mail address to the web site or list-manager. The drawback with this process is that the address could be submitted inadvertently by its owner or by a third party without the owner's consent. A double opt-in system does not add the e-mail address to the list on the first occasion, but rather triggers a message to the e-mail address itself, informing the owner that a request has been made to join the list, and soliciting a response. If no response is forthcoming, the e-mail address remains off the list. It is only added once the owner responds to the list's message, confirming that they wish to join. Members of the list have therefore had to "opt-in" twice before they are added.

The New York Times: www.nytimes.com

The well-established online news site.

New York Times Digital is the name of the Internet division that includes *NYTimes.com*, *Boston.com*, and an archive distribution business.

New York Times Digital is in the "news and information business", its mission being to "enhance society by creating the premier quality network for everyone seeking the best news, information and interaction through digital media". The audience for *NYTimes.com* is global, with 85% outside of New York City, and 20% from outside the US.

Personal Information

NYTimes.com collects personal information about its registered users when they first register on the site, including details such as household income, Zip code (for US residents), and employment information. Notice that a statement referring the reader to the privacy policy is clearly visible on the following form:

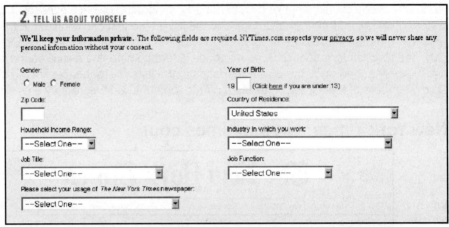

Personal information required on the registration page, with an easy to find link to the NYTimes.com privacy statement

This information is only shared with third parties (such as advertisers) in an aggregated form, giving broad demographic trends for the site, except when required by law. The personal information is also available to its owner via the membership page on the site, where users can view and modify the data, and this is further password protected (users have to enter their password even if they have the "*remember me*" cookie set).

The demographic data is categorized by @Plan, and the categories used can be viewed on the *NYTimes.com's* online media kit, at *http://www.nytimes.com/adinfo*.

User Tracking and Cookies

NYTimes.com uses cookies for authentication, tracking usage, targeting and controlling ad serving, including identifying whether a given user is allowed access to "premium" areas of the site. The terms under which this is conducted are detailed in the site's privacy statement, which includes a detailed FAQ on cookies. It is a condition of the registration process that users consent to this tracking using cookies, and again, this is clearly spelt out in the privacy policy.

The privacy policy makes clear that their advertisers also use "clear GIFS", or "Web Beacons" – we've referred to these previously as "tags" – to monitor the ad-serving systems used on the site. The policy explains that this is happening, and outlines what is involved.

Data Analysis

NYTimes.com uses an in-house log analysis system that parses the logs and reports the information, and also imports the data into an Oracle database. This allows them to conduct more specific queries on the data as the need arises. The output from the system can be in the form of HTML reports, which can be generated using a browser-based administration system, and Excel sheets and charts.

The system can track and report on:

- Usage patterns on the site
- Return visits for registered users
- Display of and response to advertising material
- Time spent by users on the site
- Visits referred from e-mails, including "*Today's Headlines*", which is sent to 3.3 million people every day
- International visitors (reported by comScore Networks)

Time spent on the site is considered to be a key indicator of visitor loyalty, and *NYTimes.com* currently leads the US news category in this respect.

NYTimes.com compared with other US news sites. Data from comScore Media Metrix

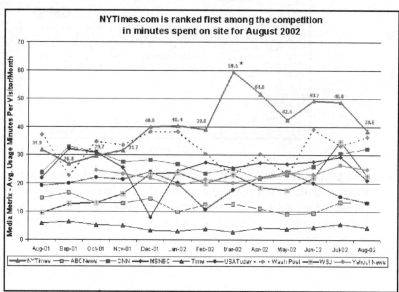

81

Opting In, Opting Out

All mailing lists on *NYTimes.com* are maintained on a strictly opt-in basis. When a new user registered, they are sent an e-mail to confirm this, and another two weeks later with additional information about the site. In the event of the user not returning to the site in a year, then they are sent one further e-mail. Membership of the mailing lists are available to the registered users via their membership page, where they can select or deselect checkboxes to join or leave each list.

Seal Programs

NYTimes.com is a member of two Seal programs, having joined TRUSTe in 1997, and BBBOnline soon afterwards. The reason for wanting to join these programs was that The New York Times is a trusted brand in print media, and it was important to continue this trust online. The Seal Programs were an excellent way of maintaining this, as they are recognized representing industry standards.

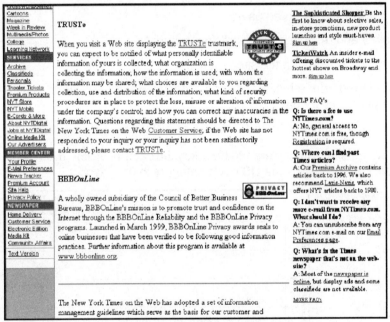

NYTimes.com Seal program membership

The process of joining the programs was straightforward, although some slight modifications to the privacy statement were implemented to ensure full compliance. As privacy is an evolving subject, constant review and revision is important. Any changes that are made to the policy must involve notification to both programs, and adjustments made based on their amendments.

Licenses from each program must be renewed annually, and approval requires the completion of a self-assessment report and questionnaire. Some time and resources are therefore required to manage the membership of the programs. *NYTimes.com* has a privacy committee with representatives from product development, marketing, PR, legal, and customer services departments, and this group meets regularly to discuss any privacy issues, industry developments, or policy changes. Online privacy is taken very seriously, and does require dedicated resources.

Summary

Privacy is increasingly important to the business of building and managing web sites as the general public (the users) become more aware of the issues and potential dangers to their privacy, and legislators begin to step in and rule on the subject. The overriding principle for the web site owner, however, is that good privacy is good business. By increasing the clarity of our privacy policies, we can increase the trust of those who use our sites, and so increase the potential for a more fruitful experience for everyone concerned, whether we are operating e-mail lists, publishing news services, or selling jam.

For this reason, it is advisable to have a privacy policy that is appropriate for our target audience. Owners of sites aimed at young children, for example, must exercise extreme care in their handling of users' information, but all sites that wish to develop a constructive relationship with their visitors (even those aimed at grown-ups) can benefit from taking privacy seriously. Many users will accept that certain information can legitimately be collected and used, to improve the site or service available, or to offer personalized content. Few web users will tolerate an incautious or dishonest attitude to their privacy rights, however, regardless of the legislation that may or may not apply.

Privacy policies should in most cases have at least the following attributes:

- It must be clearly available. This usually means at least a link from the home page of the site, and also any other page where information is being collected, such as an e-mail registration page, or an online survey.

- It must say who is the operator of the site, and particularly contact details in the event of a query or dispute regarding the site's privacy practices, including any accountability mechanisms (such as TRUSTe or BBBOnline).

- It must say what information is being collected, what purpose this information will serve, whether it will be distributed to other organizations or used for any purpose other than that for which it was submitted, and the consequences for the individual if they refuse to disclose certain information. For example, they will not be able to register for a "premium" service if they refuse to submit their postal address.

- It must say what measures the site takes to ensure the integrity and security of personal information that is stored, and the method for the individual to review, verify, and delete inaccurate or superfluous information.

- It must say which information the visitor has the right to opt out of, and which requires an opt-in (most commonly relevant to e-mail mailing lists, and the distribution of personal details to third parties or "carefully selected partners").

- It must say if cookies are used, and is so, give details. There is a lot of suspicion regarding the use of cookies, much of it unfounded, so the more explicit you can be the better. Explain what the cookie is, what it is used for, what it is NOT used for, and why it is in the user's interests to allow the cookie to be set.

- It must say where third parties are used, for example for the serving of ads on the site, or other partner programs. It must be explicit, and refer to the third parties' privacy policies if possible.

Emerging standards such as P3P are a useful tool for web site operators and users to talk to each other about privacy, but they are not a replacement for understanding the issues involved, and getting the policy right. Seal programs and similar self-regulatory schemes are another method available to us to increase trust and interaction, but again they are no replacement for understanding the needs and the concerns of our visitors, and ensuring that the requirements of the web site conform to them. Privacy is ultimately about openness.

3

Privacy

4

- Rapid analysis informing editorial decisions
- Analyzing high demand
- Discovering how people use your site

Author: Peter Comber

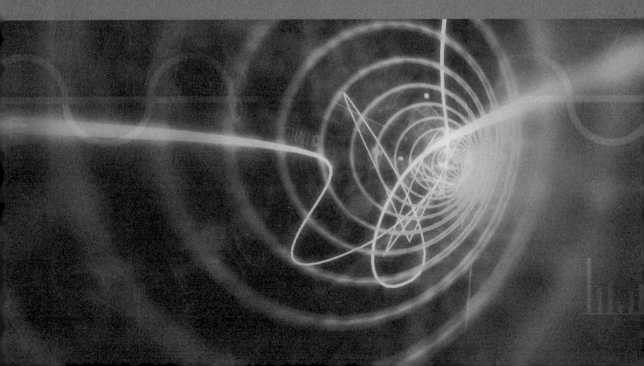

BBC News Online

It is nearly seven years since Pete Comber started working with the Internet. Having just started working in direct marketing, like most junior executives he quickly became frustrated with the fragile, incomplete, and temperamental customer databases upon which the ambitious DM strategies tended to exist. With the Internet boom in the late 1990s, he became convinced that there was massive potential for the Internet to provide large volumes of data not just about what people purchased, but about what they looked at and what they discarded, and to grant some insight into how people came to make their buying decisions. Having analyzed Internet data for four years for the UK's biggest motoring web site, he joined the BBC at the end of 2001 in the hope that he would be able to provide some useful insights into how people use the BBC News Online service.

Background and Overview

BBC *News Online* was launched in 1997 as part of the British Broadcasting Corporation's commitment to providing high-quality impartial news coverage to as wide an audience as possible. Within the larger organization, it is part of BBC News Interactive, which includes the Web and digital television output. The Web sites discussed in this chapter include BBC *News Online, Sport Online*, and *CBBC News*, a site specifically aimed at children.

In this case study we will be taking a look at the requirements of a large news and current affairs site, and demonstrating the various ways in which we approach the challenges the site and its requirements presents. Along the way, we will outline the sort of data that we collect, how we collect it, and why.

Once we have established the requirements and the methods, we will examine in detail a few of the specific elements of the site and user behavior and how we used traffic analysis to improve both the technical and editorial aspects of the site.

The BBC is principally funded by the License Fee; every household in the United Kingdom with a television is currently legally required to purchase an annual license for it. The revenue raised from this goes directly to fund the BBC. This puts us in the privileged position of being able to create a unique output of broadcast and interactive content, but of course brings with it serious responsibilities to the paying public. Advertising is not allowed in any form.

News and current affairs coverage must be impartial from a political perspective. Whilst this is a legal obligation on all television broadcasters in the UK – public, commercial, or otherwise – the BBC does have additional obligations with regard to the amount of news and current affairs programming we must produce, for example regarding the coverage of Party Political conferences.

We must try to provide something for everyone in the UK, as everyone contributes to our funding.

These strictures have specific implications for *BBC News Online*. The editors of the site must balance their judgment of what is significant in the news with the needs of our intended audience, and this is clearly a more complicated process than merely going for the most "popular" story, at the expense of those of more minority interest. The site, unlike traditional forms of news delivery, is available 24 hours a day, 365 days a year. As a result stories are being updated constantly, new ones added, and others taking a back seat. Analysis of traffic therefore needs to be accurate and up-to-date. We will see later how we are able to provide not only extremely accurate, but also very timely information to the editors.

While providing the service on a global scale is still one of our primary goals, we have a duty to those who fund the service to account for the distribution of our resources. Another consequence of the fact that the license fee is only payable by those resident in the UK is that we need to know the proportion and distribution of those using the site without contributing to our income.

From our analysis, we estimate that about 40-45% of our audience is accessing the site from outside the UK. This information is gathered from a trial that we conducted with RedSheriff, a third-party provider of tagging solutions, in which the tag is able to collect information about the regional setting of the client machine, cross-referenced with the IP address. We also conduct "reality-checks" on this data, for example by comparing it with information sent to us in feedback forms, which often include a field to indicate the country of the user.

News Online – UK version

In July 2002 we introduced two distinct versions of the site, one aimed at UK users, and the other at "World" users. The visual design of the site is the same for both versions but the balance of stories is prioritized differently for each, with the World version giving less prominence to stories that are predominantly of interest to a UK audience. Visitors are able to choose which of these two versions is their default, and are able to switch freely between the two. We use a "permanent" cookie to hold their preference between visits. (By "permanent", we mean a cookie with an expiry date set in the future – currently one year.)

News Online – World   *World Service*

As well as providing more targeted content to our audience, with news selected and highlighted to cater for the needs of our global readership, this alteration also helped to satisfy the funding issue presented by non-license payers. A significant contribution to the cost of providing the World version of the site is made by the BBC World Service, which is in turn not funded by the license fee, but by the Foreign Office, and has its own complementary brief to provide impartial and reliable information to a global audience. In fact, we believe that about 30% of the audience for the UK edition is actually accessing the site from outside of the UK.

The Traffic Information We Gather

Part of the brief for *News Online* is that it must aim to cater for the needs of all UK Internet users. Broadly speaking, those who might be regarded as our "best customers" – users who visit often, and click on a lot – can be assumed to be catered for more adequately than those who are infrequent (or non-existent) visitors. Using this information, we must redouble our efforts with regard to those who use the site least, in an attempt to provide a better or more relevant service to them. This includes providing news coverage for those who are not normally predisposed to consume news at all.

It also means that we must attempt to fill the gaps left by the commercial news services, providing coverage of topics that are destined to appeal to minority audiences. We are therefore in a rather counter-intuitive position, indeed the reverse of many commercial organizations' objectives for web traffic analysis, which is usually to focus precious resources on those most likely to reward it with regular visits, and custom.

One of the effects of this is that we must be far more cautious in our observation of the staple metric of many commercial web sites – page impressions. As we will see, page impressions are still an interesting measure of overall activity on the site, and are also a useful way for the editors to determine the relative popularity of news articles from one day to the next. When it comes to a more detailed analysis of the "success" of the site, however, we must be more circumspect, in two key respects: comparison of our page impression count with other news or content sites, and the incidence of visits which yield very few, or even just one, page impression.

ABC Electronic (ABCe) publishes the certificates on their web site (*http://www.abce.org.uk*) for every site they audit. Most of the major news sites (newspapers mainly) do audit their page impressions – so we can undertake some top-line comparisons just from there – although we do need to be careful as you are unlikely to be comparing the same months. One of the problems with this approach though is that page impressions are not an easily comparable metric, as we discuss below. Indeed, unique users are also problematic for comparisons, as there are two different measures – one using cookies and one using an IP address and user agent, which can generate wildly differing figures.

The Importance of Page Impressions

We are wholly in agreement with the principle that page impressions must have a standard definition, and indeed we ensure that ABC electronic audits our published figures. We are, however, in the rather fortunate position of not having to impress our sponsors – advertisers – with increasingly high numbers of page impressions as an indication of audience for their commercial messages. One consequence of this is that we often publish relatively long articles on a single page, whereas other sites might for a variety of perfectly good reasons (and not only the maximization of advertising revenue) need to split the article up into sections. Simply comparing our page impressions with those of a site with a different architecture and business imperative is therefore potentially highly misleading.

> *comparing page impressions with those of a site with a different architecture and business imperative is potentially highly misleading*

We have learned that most "web metrics" – including page impressions – are extremely context sensitive, and lose much of their meaning when used for a purpose other than the one for which they were originally generated. Because of this, we generate numbers for use by our editors, and we ensure that they are independently audited so that we can compare our relative growth, and the effect of significant events on our overall traffic, in a reliable manner. We would be extremely wary of using them to make anything but fairly superficial comparisons with other sites that have a different structure and different reasons for generating their numbers.

As a consequence of our need to appeal to as large a number of people as possible, we use the metric of "Reach" as a key indicator of performance. This is defined simply as the percentage of individuals in the UK with access to the Internet who have visited the site at least once in a given month, and we are currently aiming for a target of 20%. Perhaps ironically for an online source, our key metric is therefore something that is probably best measured using traditional offline market research techniques. Each month, we commission an independent market research company, BMRB, to conduct a representative survey of the UK population, and from this data determine the percentage of those with access to the Internet who visited *News Online* in the designated time period.

In the survey we only poll UK adults. According to the Office of National Statistics population estimates in mid-2000 there were 57 million people in the UK, of whom 46.5 million were adults (age 15 and over). Within our BMRB survey, which polls a representative sample of 10,000+ people per month, we ask how many of them have access to the Internet, which comes out fairly consistently at around 40%. So if there are around 18.6 million adult UK Internet users, we are aiming to get 20% of them, which works out at 3.7 million people.

Whilst this method is as imperfect as any other representative polling technique, it is nevertheless a tried and tested source of audience data, and readily comparable with other data, including the audience and Reach, for other BBC output. It is interesting to note that Internet panel surveys (for example, Nielsen Net Ratings), while perfectly valid measures in certain contexts, are not particularly relevant to the *News Online* site, as these surveys are necessarily heavily weighted towards home users. We know that the location of our UK audience is very mixed, with some home use, but also a large proportion accessing the site from the workplace.

The typical daily traffic pattern shows that traffic to the site increases steadily during the morning (UK time), with a peak at lunch time. There is a second peak to coincide with late afternoon (after work?) traffic, complemented perhaps by traffic from east coast USA coming online. This then falls away fairly sharply during the early evening.

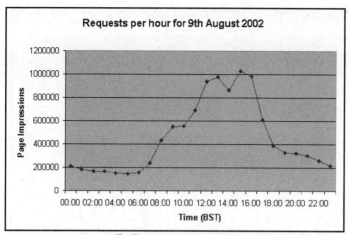

Requests per hour for 9th August 2002

Traffic on a typical day, by hour

One of the methods we use to determine where our users are visiting from is the type of connection being used to access the site. About 70% access the site through a broadband connection (probably an office network, since the domestic uptake of broadband in the UK is still relatively small). The narrow band connections (that is, via modem), which are a probable signifier of home users, account for the remaining 30%. Again, this is an intelligent assumption drawn from the data collected by RedSheriff, which is able to detect the settings in the browser to indicate the sort of connection being used.

In terms of pure traffic, the site is extremely busy, with page impressions currently at over 300 million in a typical month, and rather higher if there has been a significant news or sporting event in that period. This traffic is generated by an average of about 4 million unique users per day.

The following chart shows the dramatic increase in traffic to the site since its launch in 1997. After a steady start, traffic began to build as Internet access in the UK improved, and awareness of the BBC's interactive services took hold. It is interesting to note that "normal" traffic levels have now exceeded the sharp spike that resulted from September 11th and its aftermath.

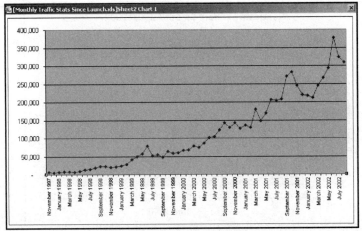

Site traffic by month since News Online launched. Page impressions are continuing to increase

Overview of Technical Architecture

The News Online web site is hosted on about 20 Apache web servers running on Linux, although the exact figure is flexible as more can be brought in at times of estimated high demand. These servers are clustered and split between two sites, one in the UK and one in the US. This split and clustered architecture is necessary to cope with the global traffic to the site, and has proven remarkably stable, holding up even against the most extreme demand.

When it was first launched, the *News* site was hosted on Microsoft IIS, but we have migrated to the current installation over the last few years. With the subsequent launch of other parts of the BBC's web presence on this platform, it made sense from the point of view of technical compatibility for *News Online* to fall in line.

Three Requirements of Our Traffic Analysis

The analysis that we do divides neatly into three distinct categories, each with its own purpose and implementation:

1. The League Table Generator: designed for our internal editorial requirements, consisting of a "league table" of page impressions for the most popular articles on the previous day.

2. Audited Log Analysis: the careful production of very accurate traffic results, which are audited and used for external reporting.

3. Detailed Visitor Analysis: used both for design and architectural changes to the site itself, and also for long-term editorial policy decisions.

League Table Generator

Every morning, our editors receive in total ten different HTML e-mails containing a "league table" of the most popular articles from each section of the site on the previous day. Behind the simple task of creating these e-mails is a very large amount of effort. The script that builds the e-mail has to process anything between 10 and 15 million page impressions, weeding out along the way all logged requests that are not valid page impressions – for example those that are not article pages, as well as any traffic generated by robots.

The work is done by three Perl scripts, and the order of work is summarized below. Perl was designed for this sort of task, involving the parsing of text strings, making it an excellent choice.

1. Just after midnight (UK time), download the compressed log files from 20 Apache web servers (typically, sometimes more) based in the UK and the US.

2. Parse each log file in turn for article pages, stripping out robot traffic by checking it against an up-to-date list of known robots and spiders, and other discountable criteria (for example, internal IP addresses, unacceptable HTTP status codes, specific file extensions; things that aren't included in the industry standards).

3. Separate all valid pages into several arrays, allowing page impression counting against edition (UK, IFS and microsite/shared) and subject (news, sport, language).

Content on the site is allocated to one of three "geographical" categories: the UK edition, the World edition (sometimes referred to as the International Facing Site, or IFS), and content that is "global", such as the World Cup coverage (a microsite, content that is shared between the principal editions).

4. Sort and combine appropriate index and default pages (for example, combine count for */1/hi/england/* and */1/hi/england/default.stm*; we'll explain this naming shortly).

5. Rank all of the articles based on total page impressions.

6. Check each CPS-generated filename in each array against the CPS database and extract the article title and section. This is done by matching up the reference number for the story (which appears in the URL in the log file) against the relevant CPS entry to extract the Headline and Section of the site for which it was originally written.

4

BBC News Online

> We use a Content Production System (CPS) – at the heart of which is a large Oracle Database containing all of the articles written for *News Online* since the site's inception in 1997.

7. For each non-CPS filename, examine the URL and try to provide a suitable title from a lookup table.

8. Generate an HTML e-mail containing the top 50 articles, and send it to the editorial team.

Due to the volume of data to be processed, the script takes several hours to run, but we aim to have the e-mail in the editors' inbox by 9am each morning. We usually achieve this target, though when the site has been especially busy the day before, they sometimes have to wait a few extra minutes.

The e-mails generated by this system contain the following information:

- Date. Occasionally e-mails may appear on a following day, if the system fails for some reason. Also, people do tend to hang on to them for a few days for reference, so a clear indication of what day they are looking at is important.

- Total traffic to the *news.bbc.co.uk* domain. This includes sport, some foreign language content, children's news, and a few other related sections. In itself this is something of an academic measure, but it is one of the only ones that has been consistently recorded since the site launched, so it is useful for monitoring trends in site growth.

- Breakdown of traffic by (geographical) edition. In this case, looking at news content only. The three editions of the site are set out as follows: UK edition, International edition, and Non-Specific, which contains Features as well as some archive content published before the site was split between the UK and International editions.

- For each edition we give a total for that edition of the site. We then split out the number of page impressions of specific articles from the index pages. We used to report indexes, but don't any more as these constituted a large proportion of the top 50 pages on the site, preventing editors from seeing what the top articles for the day were, and therefore defeating the purpose of the e-mail. Consequently, index pages are filtered out from the top 50 pages that are reported here.

The following screenshots show the top 50 articles for the UK and International editions (respectively) on August 28, 2002. They also contain a summary of the totals for each of the three editions detailed above.

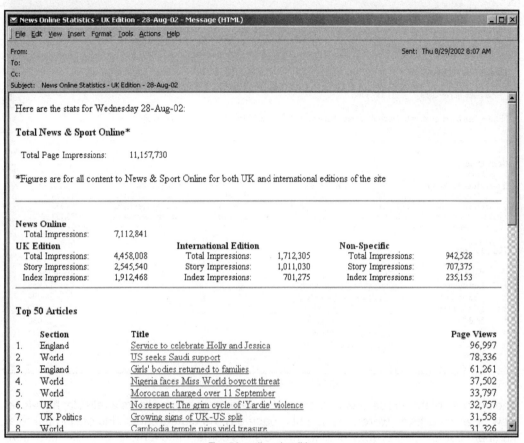

Top 50 mail – uk edition

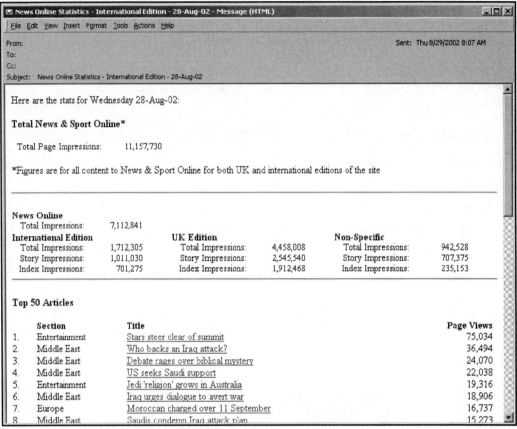

News Online Statistics - International Edition - 28-Aug-02 - Message (HTML)

File   Edit   View   Insert   Format   Tools   Actions   Help

From: Sent: Thu 8/29/2002 8:07 AM
To:
Cc:
Subject: News Online Statistics - International Edition - 28-Aug-02

Here are the stats for Wednesday 28-Aug-02:

Total News & Sport Online*

   Total Page Impressions: 11,157,730

*Figures are for all content to News & Sport Online for both UK and international editions of the site

News Online
   Total Impressions: 7,112,841

International Edition		UK Edition		Non-Specific	
Total Impressions:	1,712,305	Total Impressions:	4,458,008	Total Impressions:	942,528
Story Impressions:	1,011,030	Story Impressions:	2,545,540	Story Impressions:	707,375
Index Impressions:	701,275	Index Impressions:	1,912,468	Index Impressions:	235,153

Top 50 Articles

	Section	Title	Page Views
1.	Entertainment	Stars steer clear of summit	75,034
2.	Middle East	Who backs an Iraq attack?	36,494
3.	Middle East	Debate rages over biblical mystery	24,070
4.	Middle East	US seeks Saudi support	22,038
5.	Entertainment	Jedi 'religion' grows in Australia	19,316
6.	Middle East	Iraq urges dialogue to avert war	18,906
7.	Europe	Moroccan charged over 11 September	16,737
8.	Middle East	Saudis condemn Iraq attack plan	15,273

Top 50 mail – International edition

The purpose of this process is very straightforward: to give our editors a reliable, high-level view of which articles were most popular each day. As stated earlier, increasing the total number of article page views, or steering the site's content into a more "populist" direction, is not our priority, but clearly a reliable picture of how our readers are reacting to the content on offer is an essential tool to have at the editors' disposal.

While it is obviously important that the data summarized in these daily reports is accurate, its primary purpose is for internal decision-making, and, as *News Online* is updated every minute of the day, speed is an equally crucial factor. Consequently, the filtering process whereby logs are parsed and stripped of robot traffic is somewhat "quick and dirty" (although we do still use the same "exclusion criteria" as the ABCe audited data), as we strike a compromise between functionality and accuracy. In practice, however, the report is remarkably accurate, with only a 5% margin of error compared with our officially audited figures.

" increasing the total number of article page views, or steering the site's content into a more "populist" direction, is not our priority "

Audited Log Analysis

As the BBC is an organization funded by the public, through the license fee, we must take our reporting responsibilities very seriously. For this reason we have signed up with ABC electronic to audit the reporting of our traffic analysis. ABCe supply us with a valid list of known robots every month, and it is this list that is used when we compile our official audience numbers for public distribution. The auditing process also involves overseeing the way in which we collect, clean, and summarize our data, ensuring that we conform with currently accepted standards, and that the numbers generated are as meaningful as possible to those outside of the BBC.

As ABCe's industry agreed standards are necessarily very strict, we use a different method to produce our audited figures from the one used to generate the "overnight" numbers discussed in the previous section.

The principal tool we use for our audited traffic numbers is Analog. This program is ideal for us, as it is very good at parsing large quantities of data, and – crucially for auditing purposes – it does not attempt to embellish the statistical information by making assumptions about what the log information means, particularly in terms of individual "visits", or other more qualitative judgments about our users' behavior.

Analog is not only a very efficient program, but it is also open source, meaning that we are free to use it and adapt it to our specific needs. (The fact that it is also free in a financial sense is beneficial to our license payers too, of course.) We will see shortly how we have been able to use Analog, in conjunction with the cookie data captured in the log files, to give us a very reliable indication of unique users, another metric that is audited by ABCe.

 ensure that URLs have a logical and readable structure We are able to adjust the settings in Analog's configuration file to ensure that it is aware of the structure of the site, and it allows us to customize the output to our requirements.

Here it is interesting to note that, due to an earlier decision made about the directory structure of News Online (in short, to ensure that URLs have a logical and readable structure), we can generate detailed reports on each section of the site rather easily. Take as an example the following URL for an article about the effect managers have been having on the UK economy: *http://news.bbc.co.uk/1/hi/business/2228274.stm*.

- */1* means this page is from the UK version of the site. The World version would have a */2*.

- */hi* means this is a "high graphics" version. The alternative would be /low.

- */business* means the news section where this story was created, other examples include */education, /science,* or */entertainment*. This part can sometimes be subdivided again, into distinct topic areas of the particular department, for example */entertainment/film*.

- /2228274.stm indicates the file itself, based on the unique identifier for each article in our database.

Given this neat and regular structure, it is fairly straightforward to configure Analog to produce traffic reports with the data broken down by site version, department, topic, and so on.

As we are using Apache, it would be possible to instruct the LogDirectives to not log robot traffic; however, due to the high volume nature of the site, it is more efficient to have it parsed out later, hence our approach.

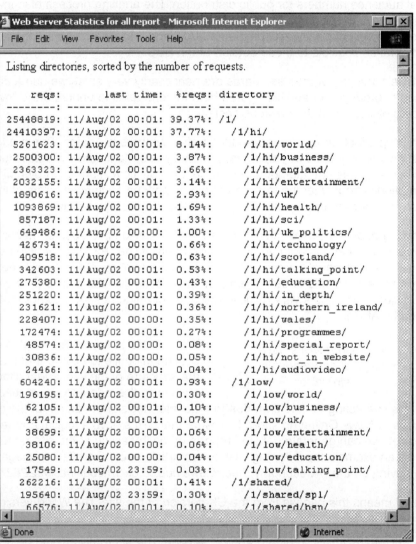

Analog traffic report by site version

It is also essential that we are able to exclude from the traffic data all known robot activity, and Analog allows us to supply it with a list of robots in the configuration file. We insert here ABCe's latest list of known robots.

Use of Cookies

We use cookies to allow us to track users anonymously on all BBC web sites. All BBC sites that are set up as subdomains of bbc.co.uk are able to use the same cookie, thus enabling us to collect data on users' activity across a whole family of sites. This is very important, as the internal distinctions that form the boundaries between our sites are often of little interest to visitors to the site, and there are numerous hyperlinks from one site to another.

Cookies are set using a custom-built Apache module. This gives us a very efficient method of setting the cookie, and one that is highly customizable to our specific requirements. The cookie setting system uses the following logic:

1. A request is received, and the module checks to see if it contains a BBC cookie.

2. If there is no cookie present, then the module sends a new cookie in the response, and this cookie is "flagged" as a temporary "1st cookie". The cookie contains a long "token", an alphanumeric string including random elements, designed to identify the user (or at least their browser) uniquely, though anonymously.

3. If the cookie received in the request is one which has been flagged in this way, then it indicates that this is a "new" user (their second request to the site), and a new cookie is sent in the response, but it is not flagged as temporary: it is set with an expiry date of one year in the future. The "new" cookie contains the original token, thus maintaining the identity of the user, and it is this cookie we are interested in.

4. If the cookie received is not flagged as temporary, then it is sent back with the request, but again with the expiry date set to one year.

This system will under-count unique users to the extent that some people may only visit once, and not come back before their cookie expires. This fact is not particularly significant, however, partly because the actual number of users in this category is small, but more particularly because the point of the cookie system is to be able to gather data on session use patterns, and return rates. Users who visit the site once before the cookie expires are not therefore relevant to this research in any case.

Detailed Visitor Analysis

The third requirement we have for our traffic analysis is to provide detailed information on visitor activity, not only for our editors, but also for the design team, who can use what we find to improve functionality and usability on the site. For this analysis, we use a third-party product called NetGenesis, and it works as follows:

1. The log files from *News Online* are loaded into the NetGenesis system.

2. NetGenesis then "cleans" files (for example, by removing robot traffic).

3. The clean data is then inserted into the NetGenesis database.

4. A sophisticated NetGenesis web user interface allows us to make detailed queries on the data and reports the results.

After an extensive discussion, we have decided that there is only one robot and filtering list that will be used across the BBC systems. The list is largely based on that supplied to us by ABCe. There are also a few conventions about which pages we are going to measure and which we don't (which count as "pages"), and these get added on to the ABCe suppression list. We don't add on any additional robots though – even if we know there are some out there. This is mainly in order to help keep the data comparable with other audited sites, and to ensure that everyone is using the same rulebook.

NetGenesis actually uses its own filtering system, which we do have to keep more of an eye on manually. For this system we simply monitor the traffic data compared to the two other systems to ensure it does not fall out of line – in practice it rarely does.

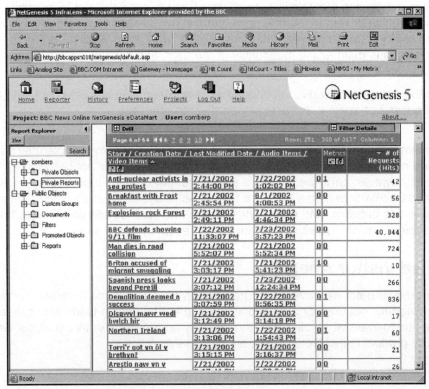

NetGenesis report

Most of the work that we do with NetGenesis involves tracking (anonymous) visitors' activity on the site, and it is therefore dependent on the use of cookies. Whilst this will naturally exclude a small proportion of our users from this analysis (those who visit the site with their "accept cookie" option turned off) this system is still very useful in giving us detailed qualitative information about our users' behavior.

By definition if the visitor has switched the accept cookie option off then we cannot really identify the number of 'users' affected. We do monitor the discrepancy between the number of pages that have a legitimate cookie and the number where there is either no cookie, or the cookie is flagged as temporary, as defined above. In general the proportion without a permanent cookie is about 10% of pages. Our main concern is that this level remains constant – and broadly speaking it does – so the underlying traffic trends are always faithfully reflected.

As the work that NetGenesis does is very detailed (we will look at an example of this shortly), we have to handle the issue of the sheer volume of data that we collect. Indeed, it would be extremely slow and

> *we are looking for qualitative information – not detailed analysis on every single visitor to the site, but rather a representative sample*

unwieldy to load all of our data into the NetGenesis system. Here we take advantage of the fact that we are looking for qualitative information – after all, we are not looking to do detailed analysis on every single visitor to the site, but rather a representative sample. We therefore operate a polling technique to give us the sample we can work with more easily.

When NetGenesis loads the data from the log files into its database, it checks the last digit of the randomly allocated token in the cookie. It will then only load the data related to that cookie if a given digit is a 5 or a 0 (for example), thus giving us a randomly selected 20% sample from the complete set of data. This figure of 20% is both a large enough sample for the work we do to be representative, but also a small enough quantity of data for the system to work efficiently, without becoming weighed down with data that we will never use. We believe that this polling technique is an elegant solution to the problem of resolving the real-world needs of our organization (accurate statistics) with the practical problems that this entails (high volume of data).

Drilling Down into User Behavior: The One-Hit Wonder Phenomenon

> *page impressions are a complex metric: sometimes "less is more"*

I have discussed earlier the idea that page impressions are a complex metric: sometimes "less is more". To illustrate this, let's look more deeply at a practical illustration: the phenomenon of the one-page visit.

Detailed analysis reveals that we receive a number of single requests for the home page, which are then not followed up by that user in the form of repeated requests. We also know that this user might return frequently, sometimes several times a day, but rarely ventures further than the first page. The initial findings about the large number of visits to *News Online* yielding only the one page impression was found using the NetGenesis analysis tool – where a frighteningly large proportion of people only seemed to see one page.

For a site which is required to be as "sticky" as possible, this sort of user might appear something of a disappointment, resulting in meetings and design briefings designed to figure out how to persuade them to stay longer, and consume more content on the site. Whilst this is reasonable analysis for sites that require multiple page views for their business model, it is not necessarily a problem for *News Online*.

We place a lot of useful information on the home page, principally headlines and short summaries of the current leading news stories. We know from market research and focus group research into the requirements of a "news audience" that many people are primarily looking for a headline service. In the case of an online news source, they visit simply to check what is happening "out there", and, having found the information that they required, they leave satisfied. Given our brief, this is a perfectly acceptable result for us, as we are providing those users with precisely the service that they require, and on the occasions that a headline captures their interest, the detail is available deeper into the site.

This was one site where you didn't need to go clicking through hundreds of pages to find out what was going on in the world

In order to examine this belief in more detail, we looked into it a bit deeper the next time we carried out some focus group research into the site.

We set people the task of comparing different news sites, and one of the positive comments which kept on coming up about News Online was the fact that you could actually get a pretty good overview of the day's events just by looking at the home page. This was one site where you didn't need to go clicking through hundreds of pages to find out what was going on in the world – and was something that got resounding thumbs up across many of the groups that we ran.

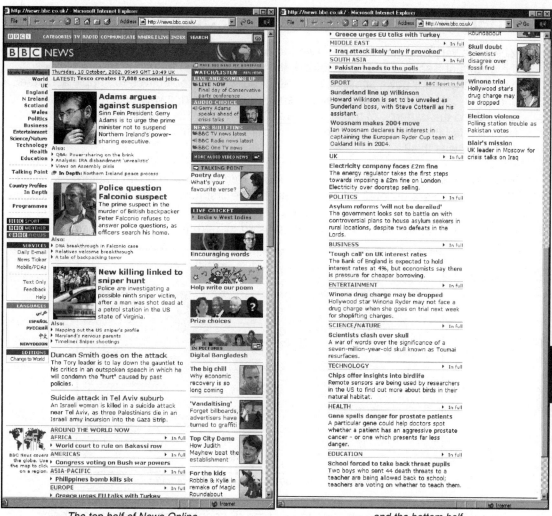

The top half of News Online...　　　　　　　*...and the bottom half*

For these people, generating a large number of page impressions when accessing the site was actually a negative user experience, when ironically we would have been congratulating ourselves for the increases in traffic we were cleverly generating. This is therefore a great example of how traditional metrics are useful for assessing the "performance" of a site, but without a detailed understanding of the needs of your user, a simplistic approach to such metrics can be unhelpful, or downright misleading.

Analyzing Extreme Demand: September 11, 2001

It became very apparent to those trying to access news information on the Web that as the events of September 11th unfolded, the global demand for information effectively disabled the major news sites. As it is one of our primary objectives to supply accurate and up-to-date information on major events, as they unfold, it was essential that we understood the patterns of traffic to *News Online* during this time. Detailed analysis in fact revealed that September 11th was not our highest traffic day – it was September 12th. Why was this?

The first plane hit the north tower of the World Trade Center at 08:46 Eastern Standard Time. Our logs are maintained on UK time, so the first news of the attack was posted on the site shortly before 2pm (BST) in the UK. In effect therefore, by the time demand began to surge, over half of the day had passed as normal.

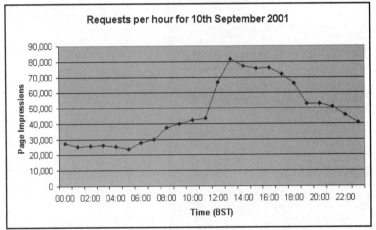

September 10, 2001: a normal day of site traffic

While it is technically true to say that the site was still up-and-running, this would be a slightly disingenuous claim as, due to all of the IP connections to the Internet being "full", visitors could not access the site. From a user's point of view it makes no difference: we were unable to supply the necessary information. Having hit a "glass ceiling" in our capacity, the actual traffic on the site would be limited, but as the site did not technically break, the servers continued to log traffic.

Traffic to the site remained extremely high overnight – which is why the figure for the 12th is higher. We believe that this was predominantly US-generated traffic, as the BBC was probably the most widely used non-American site when US sites were overwhelmed by the traffic. This would have been helped by the fact that, as the site is written in English, a number of US portals (for example, Google) were referring people to News Online as a source on the events as they unfolded.

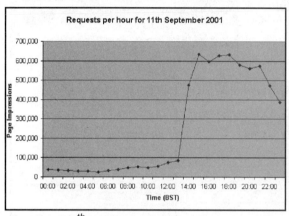

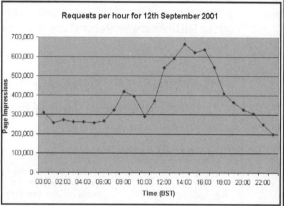

September 11th, 2001: the day starts normally, but surges from 2pm onwards

September 12th, 2001: the curve is similar to a normal day, only the figures are much higher

News Service or Archive Service?

News Online has a vast and growing archive of articles documenting events in the UK and the rest of the world, written by respected and independent journalists. This archive is a treasure, which should certainly be preserved for future research and reference purposes, but how much is it accessed on a day-to-day basis on the web site?

There was an assumption that, as the archive of articles was both so rich and so large, there must be a huge number of page impressions drawn from this part of the site. Therefore, in order to correctly prioritize our work, and improve usability based on actual user requirements, we undertook a detailed survey to determine the real patterns of use.

Initial findings indicated that 80% of all of the articles in our archive were accessed at least once in any given month. Once this was reported, however, it soon became distorted into the belief that **80% of all of our page impressions came from the archive**. Whilst this is a relatively small semantic shift, and typical of the sort of mutation that statistics undergo as they pass around large organizations, it actually represents a fundamentally different phenomenon than was actually being observed. It is worth delving a little deeper into what we ultimately discovered in order to illustrate the importance of precision when discussing web metrics, as well as the extent to which any given metric is highly context-sensitive, or ripe for misinterpretation.

The exact definition of an "archived" article, as opposed to a "live" one, is necessarily ambiguous. In practice, articles tend to slip into the archive after two or three days as they cease to be linked to directly from one of the main index pages on the site, and as the specific news story fades and is supplanted by newer items. The tailing off of a news story is incredibly marked, with a severe "L" shaped life cycle, with almost all of its page impressions coming in the first two days, and then a prolonged period of flat demand. This article about REM member Peter Buck is typical:

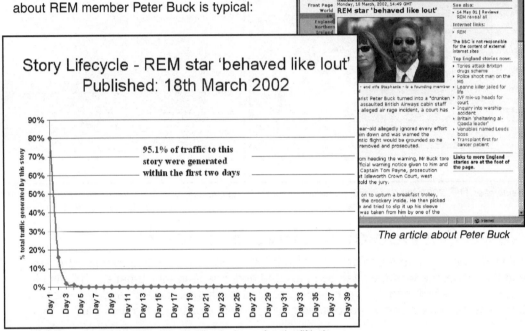

The article about Peter Buck

The life cycle of the article – practically no views after the fifth day

Detailed examination of traffic patterns, principally using the NetGenesis tool, revealed that around 80% of all page impressions on the site (excluding index pages) are to articles that are less than three days old, contrary to the previous belief that the archive was generating the majority of traffic.

Summary

The *News Online* site is huge, both in terms of its total volume of content, and the number of page impressions generated per day. This reality, coupled with the fact that we operate a 24-hour news service every day of the year, means that accurate traffic analysis is both essential, and a major challenge. What lessons can be leaned from the methods that we use?

The first point is that we do not rely on a single method of analysis, but use three different analysis techniques that are at least in part independent of each other, and the results are compared and cross-referenced for anomalies. This is also important because different people within the organization use the traffic analysis for different purposes, and the one-size-fits-all approach would be inadequate. Therefore we have our own custom scripts for an overnight snapshot, an established analysis tool (Analog) for our audited figures, and a specialist third-party solution (NetGenesis) for detailed data-mining work. We are always looking to improve our knowledge, and this is why we have been conducting trials of other solutions, such as client tagging, and comparing the results with what we already believe.

This multi-method approach, however, leads us on to a final warning message. While one of the purposes of web traffic analysis is to compare the performance and use of our site with others on the Web, any comparisons must be taken extremely carefully. Different sites produce their figures in subtly different ways: even comparing sites audited by the same organization can mislead too superficial a glance at the numbers under review. There are different techniques for calculating the key measures, such as unique users, and even measures that are statistically consistent, such as page impressions, can be misleading if the sites being compared have different notions of why they are counting these pages.

We put a lot of effort and serious thought into our traffic analysis, but we treat it with care. Each piece of information can be extremely useful to part of our operation, but we are cautious about reading too much into any individual element, and ensure that we view it in the context in which it was devised. So long as we adhere to this rule, our traffic analysis can remain an important part of both the technical and the editorial development of the site.

4

BBC News Online

5

- Segmenting pages
- Finding bottlenecks in the site
- Anonymously tracking random visitors

Author: Alex Poon

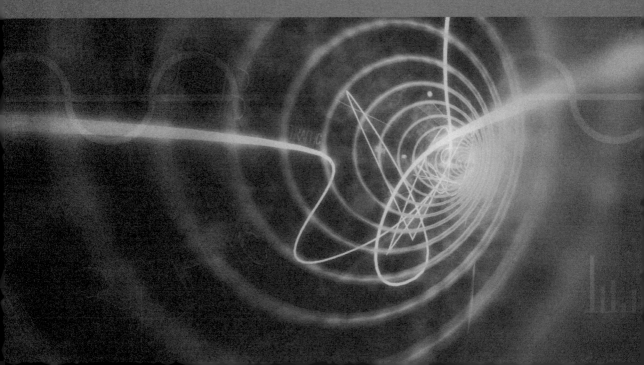

eBay

Alex Poon was one of the first engineers at eBay, and started off as the de facto "UI guy" back in 1997. He started eBay's first user-interface group at eBay in 1999, then later ran eBay's Advanced Technologies Group, during which his team implemented eBay's first web traffic analysis system. Although Alex recently left eBay after five years, he was happy to describe its traffic analysis process in his own words.

What is eBay?

eBay, as you probably know, is an online marketplace where millions of people from around the world come together to buy and sell goods from one another. Sellers list items for sale either in an auction-style format, in which the item goes to the highest bidder after a preset period of time (usually seven days), or in a fixed-price format in which the first buyer who is willing to pay a specified price "wins" the item. In the auction-style format, *eBay* sends e-mail to bidders who have been outbid, giving them the opportunity to increase their bids before the auction ends. Once a winner has been determined, *eBay* sends notices to the seller and the winning bidder, notifying them of the results, and instructing them on the next steps to complete the transaction. The buyer sends payment to the seller, the seller ships the item directly to the buyer, and finally, the seller and buyer post either positive or negative feedback comments in a public forum for others to see.

Sounds simple, does it not? Well, it is indeed simple, and in fact *eBay* began in 1995 as a tiny web site run by just a single engineer, Pierre Omidyar, as a part-time hobby. It was a big hit with folks from the beginning, and Pierre soon learned that the concept was not only simple, but also addictive and even profitable. *eBay* has now exploded to become the most successful purely-online business in the world, with over 50 million buyers and sellers worldwide, transacting over $5 billion in the year 2000.

How eBay Makes Money

Unlike most online retail shopping sites, *eBay* does not hold inventory or collect money from buyers. Instead, *eBay* charges a small listing fee per item for sellers to list their items for sale, and once a listed item sells successfully, *eBay* charges a final value fee which is calculated as a percentage of the selling price. *eBay* also offers additional services and features, such as the ability for a seller to feature their item on *eBay*'s homepage, the ability to display thumbnail gallery images next to a seller's item listings, and the ability for a seller to set up a permanent store on *eBay*. Though *eBay*'s revenue is generated almost exclusively from the sellers and not the buyers, basic economics tells us that without buyers to bid on sellers' items, sellers will not list items for sale. Because of this fact, you will see later in this chapter that we focus our web traffic analysis not only on the selling processes, but also on the buying processes as well.

Why eBay Needs Web Traffic Analysis

You would think that as one of the largest Internet sites, with over 10 billion page views per month, *eBay* would have put into place sophisticated tracking mechanisms early on to measure and analyze its traffic. However, it was not until 2001, six years after inception, that a small team of engineers put into place a real system for measuring site activity. Though we had collected ordinary web server logs long before then, they were not nearly sufficient for what we really needed to learn about our site, and our current system goes far beyond the parsing of web server logs. In designing our web traffic analysis system, we started out by identifying five high-level needs:

Technographic data describes the technologies that end users have on their computers, such as browser types, screen sizes, and plug-ins

- Measuring the completion rate of key processes

- Measuring the effectiveness of marketing initiatives

- Measuring the effectiveness of searching and browsing techniques

- Gathering technographic data

- Gathering anonymous visitor data

We will look at each of these in detail now.

Measuring the Completion Rate of Key Processes

How often do users begin the registration process but do not actually finish it? How often do sellers begin listing an item for sale, become confused or frustrated, and exit the site? It might be hard to believe, but we did not have the ability to collect data about such key sequences on the site until we implemented our current web traffic analysis system. Not only is it important for us to use these metrics to monitor the usability of the site, but it is also equally important for measuring the return on investment for any changes to such features. For instance, in 2002 we completely revamped the *Sell Your Item* page flow, changing it from a single, lengthy form, to a multi-page wizard process. The web traffic analysis system allowed us to measure whether the change was actually beneficial (more on that later in this chapter).

Measuring the Effectiveness of Marketing Initiatives

The front page of eBay. The eBay™ Mark is a trademark of eBay™ Inc. eBay™ screenshots used by permission of eBay™ Inc.

As almost all shopping sites do, *eBay*'s homepage and category portal pages contain several tantalizing marketing messages, encouraging users to click and dig deeper into the site:

The folks in the usability group at *eBay* and the marketing groups go back and forth on how much page real estate to devote to these marketing links. On the one hand, the usability group argues that the more links we have, the more cluttered the page, thereby making it less likely that users will click on any one of them. On the other hand, the marketing folks believe that a greater diversity of links will appeal to a greater proportion of the user community. Web traffic analysis allows us to determine empirically not only the right number of links, but also which marketing links are most popular.

Measuring the Effectiveness of Searching and Browsing

When users arrive at the *eBay* homepage, what do they do immediately next? Thanks to web traffic analysis, we now know the answer: most users either type in search keywords to narrow down quickly the list of products in which they are interested, or click on one of the main categories to browse more methodically through specific categories. But web traffic analysis can go much further than simply informing us which links and features are most popular; it can also inform us which ones are most effective in producing the outcome that benefits the community of sellers the most, namely bidding. Later, I will take you through an in-depth look into how we use web traffic analysis to determine which types of searching and browsing are most likely to result in a user bidding.

Gathering Technographic Data

Technology improves, new browsers and operating systems appear in the marketplace, and users upgrade their systems. These changes allow us to make the *eBay* experience richer and simpler (hopefully!), but adopting new technologies runs the risk of alienating folks who do not upgrade to the latest and greatest. For instance, technologies such as JavaScript, Java, and Flash, while allowing a richer set of user-interface elements, are not supported by 100% of users' systems. Similarly, while most users now have screens that can display 1024x768 pixels or more, many still have 800x600 displays. Web traffic analysis can not only inform us of what percentage of the user community support a particular technology, but can also show us the rate at which the user community adopts new technologies. Having technographic data allows us to optimize the site for the majority, yet still make eBay accessible to those in the technical minority.

Gathering Anonymous Visitor Statistics

Web server logs give us statistics about how many page views the site gets per day; however, we also need to know how many unique visitors we receive per day, how often they return to the site, and how deep into the site users go on average. On top of that, we also measure how these statistics are broken up by country, as it is especially important for our new country sites to understand the growth rate and how it relates to our advertising efforts.

eBay's Web Traffic Analysis System

With the above needs in mind, we sought to design a system that would be easy to deploy, cost-efficient, and that would satisfy the goals above. In this section, I will describe the specific requirements we needed for our web traffic analysis system, explain why we chose a client-side JavaScript solution to satisfy those requirements, and give a detailed technical description of how the system really works.

Requirements

Our first steps involved translating our high-level goals to specific web traffic analysis feature requirements. The features we decided that we needed were page view reports, unique visitor reports, page flow analysis, technographic reports, and page property reports.

Page View Reports

The most basic report that we needed, and I would think that any web site would want, is one that shows on a daily basis, the number of page views that each unique page on the site receives. Though it sounds like a simple requirement, there is an important nuance that makes it less straightforward than you would think. On almost all modern web sites, including *eBay*'s, the pages on the site are not all static – rather, they are generated dynamically in real-time using ISAPI (Internet Server Application Programming Interface) or J2EE (Java 2 Platform Enterprise Edition), and therefore can change each time a user views a page. For example, on *eBay*, every item listed for sale has its own page, called the *ViewItem* page. At a given time, there are tens of millions of items listed for sale on the eBay site, which of course means that there are tens of millions unique *ViewItem* pages that could be potentially tracked in the page view reports. On top of that, each *ViewItem* page changes over time, to reflect the current price, number of bidders, and the time left to bid. Here the trick is deciding what constitutes a unique page, and therefore warrants having its own unique page name shown in the page view reports.

At one extreme, not only could each of the tens of millions of *ViewItem* pages be considered unique, but also every time a *ViewItem* page changes it could be considered a new page. At the other extreme, we could lump all ViewItem pages together as one unique page. The problem with this approach is that you then lose the ability to count *ViewItem* pages for individual product categories (for example, you may want to know how many ViewItem pages were viewed in the Sporting Goods category versus the Trading Cards category). As you will see later, we strike a balance by introducing a concept called **page properties** that allows us to track page views and particular properties of pages separately.

Note that the page name we are referring to here is what shows up in the web traffic analysis reports – it is not the actual filename of the page on eBay's filesystem.

Because we did not want to lock ourselves into doing it a certain way forever, we required that whatever system we put into place would allow us easily to change page names down the road. And, in fact, we have taken advantage of that requirement several times since launch. For instance, we initially decided that all *ViewItem* pages would be lumped under the name "ViewItem", regardless of the time left in the auction. Later, we realized that if an auction had ended, it made sense to track views to that auction's *ViewItem* page differently. The change was easy – we simply re-tagged ended *auction* pages to be named *ViewItemEnded*.

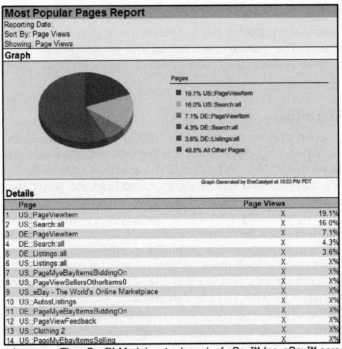

eBay's most popular pages. The eBay™ Mark is a trademark of eBay™ Inc. eBay™ screenshots used by permission of eBay™ Inc.

The above figure shows an example of a page view report. Notice that we begin every page name with the country abbreviation, so that we can easily distinguish between same-named pages of different country sites.

Unique Visitor Reports

In addition to page view counts, almost everyone interested in web traffic analysis is interested in unique visitor counts, and *eBay* is no exception. However, as discussed in *Chapter 1*, unique visitor reports are inherently inaccurate, in that they cannot guarantee that each reported unique visitor is actually a unique person. Still, we felt that these reports were necessary, because they are useful for monitoring growth trends, and comparing unique visitor counts across similar subsites.

The most general requirement we could have set would be one in which we could collect unique visitor counts for any subset of pages of the entire *eBay* site (for example, tallying the unique visitors to a single page or single feature of the site). However, we realized later that each subset of pages for which we wanted to track unique visitors would require its own cookie.

Because browsers limit cookies to twenty per domain, and we already use cookies for reasons other than web traffic analysis (such as user logins), we realized early on that such a general requirement could be difficult. Therefore, in the end, we made a simple requirement of tracking unique visitors by subsite, rather than any set of arbitrary pages, in order to stay within the twenty-cookie limit.

Page Flow Analysis

One of the main reasons that we decided to implement a web traffic analysis system was for page flow analysis. More specifically, for every page on the *eBay* site, we wanted the ability to see how users got to that page, and where users went after it. This data is useful not only for measuring completion rates of key processes on the site, but also for uncovering the problem areas. If we were to find, for instance, that a large percentage of users get stuck at the third page of the selling process and end up hitting the *Back* button to return to the second page, then we would know to focus user-interface improvements on the third page. Page flow analysis is also useful for learning how users find key features, such as registration. For instance, before we implemented our web traffic analysis system, we had always assumed that most folks found the registration page from the *eBay* homepage. With page flow analysis reports, we now know that most users find the registration page from the bidding page, and many also find it from the sign-in page. This sort of information has proven invaluable for adjusting both the layout of our pages and the information architecture of the site.

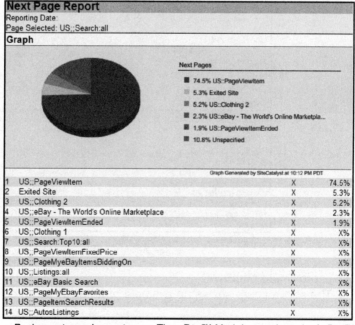

eBay's most popular next page. The eBay™ Mark is a trademark of eBay™ Inc. eBay™ screenshots used by permission of eBay™ Inc.

The previous figure shows an example of an *eBay* "next page" report for the *eBay* search page. Note that the report also shows how often users exit the site from this page.

Technographic Reports

Our requirement for technographic data was simple. We wanted browser data, operating system breakdowns, cookie acceptance data, JavaScript support, Java support, and screen size data. Most web traffic analysis packages come standard with such reports, and use a variety of methods to deduce what technologies end users have in place. For instance, browser-type data is easily gathered by parsing the USER_AGENT environment variable that all browsers send, cookie acceptance can be deduced by attempting to set a cookie and reading it back again, and screen sizes can be calculated by reading JavaScript variables. Because some technographic reports can actually depend on the existence of another technology (deducing screen size relies on the existence of JavaScript and use of version 4.0+ browsers), the reported numbers are never 100% accurate, but we understood that and were fine with getting

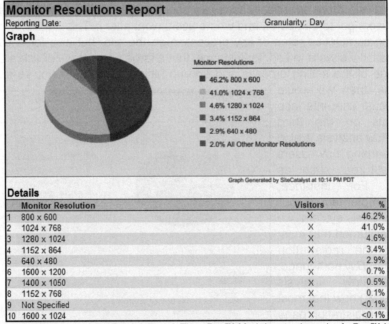

Reported resolutions at which eBay is viewed, The eBay™ Mark is a trademark of eBay™ Inc. eBay™ screenshots used by permission of eBay™ Inc.

approximate numbers.

The above figure shows an example of an *eBay* screen size report.

Page Property Reports

Everyone has heard of the 80-20 rule. For page views at *eBay*, the 80-20 rule is an understatement — in fact, over 95% of page views come from less than 5% of the pages. eBay users tend to use only a small set of pages on a regular basis, and so we wanted to track those pages in more detail than others. We came up with a concept called page properties that gives us this extra detail. Recall that earlier we discussed

> *For page views at eBay, the 80-20 rule is an understatement in fact, over 95% of page views come from less than 5% of the pages.*

the importance of naming the *ViewItem* page properly so that we could distinguish between views of items whose listings had ended versus views of items whose listings were still ongoing.By naming the pages differently, the page view reports show different line items for each of those pages. We could easily have taken that a step further, and, say, appended the category name to the page name, so that the page name might look something like *ViewItem:SportingGoods* or *ViewItem:Stamps*. However, the problem with creating unique page names for every variation of a *ViewItem* page is that not only do the reports become less readable, but also it becomes much harder to analyze the *ViewItem* page as a whole.

This is where page properties come in. We required that for the most important pages of our site (such as for *ViewItem*) we have the ability to track not only the number of page views in aggregate to that page, but also the number of page views for up to twenty different properties of that page. To continue our example, one of the twenty properties is the product category in which a viewed item resides. This way, not only could we report the number of *ViewItem* page views, but also get a breakdown of how many page views to *ViewItem* we were getting to each product category.

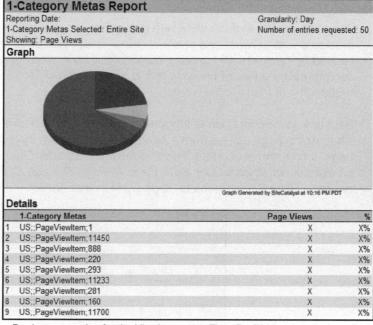

1-Category Metas Report

Reporting Date:
1-Category Metas Selected: Entire Site
Showing: Page Views

Granularity: Day
Number of entries requested: 50

Graph

Graph Generated by SiteCatalyst at 10:16 PM PDT

Details

	1-Category Metas	Page Views	%
1	US;;PageViewItem;1	X	X%
2	US;;PageViewItem;11450	X	X%
3	US;;PageViewItem;888	X	X%
4	US;;PageViewItem;220	X	X%
5	US;;PageViewItem;293	X	X%
6	US;;PageViewItem;11233	X	X%
7	US;;PageViewItem;281	X	X%
8	US;;PageViewItem;160	X	X%
9	US;;PageViewItem;11700	X	X%

Product categories for the ViewItem page. The eBay™ Mark is a trademark of eBay™ Inc. eBay™ screenshots used by permission of eBay™ Inc.

Another example of a page property that we needed was the time left in an auction. By recording how much time was left on an auction whenever a *ViewItem* page was viewed, we could run a report that showed how many views to *ViewItem* occur during the last day of an auction, versus the first day of an auction.

The previous figure shows an example of the page property report that shows the breakdown of product categories for the ViewItem page. Notice that we use category numbers rather than category names in the reports, so that the reports would be insensitive to later changes in our category names.

Client-Side JavaScript

In Chapter 1 you read about the different data-collection methodologies for web traffic analysis, including server log analysis, panel surveys, and client-side JavaScript. As I mentioned before, we at *eBay* have long used server logs to monitor traffic loads, but for achieving the goals outlines above, we needed something far more comprehensive. For that, we chose a third-party service solution named SiteCatalyst from a company called Omniture, formerly known as MyComputer (*http://www.omniture.com/*). SiteCatalyst uses basic client-side JavaScript as its technology for collecting the data, but we at *eBay* worked with the Omniture folks to add additional features not included in the initial service. While there are many companies that provide enterprise-level web traffic analysis, we chose Omniture because of their willingness to create and modify features specific to *eBay*'s needs.

The main reason that we went with a JavaScript approach was to take into account problems with browser and proxy caching. Recall that page views of pages that are cached by browsers and proxies do not show up in web server logs because the web servers have no way of knowing that a user viewed a particular page if a physical request is not made to the server.

Because JavaScript code is triggered whenever a user views a page, regardless of whether the page comes from a cache or directly from the originating web server, every page impression is counted. This is especially important for path flow analyses. Consider an example in which a user visits *Page A, Page B, Page C*, uses the back button to return to *Page B*, then goes to *Page D*, all in that order.

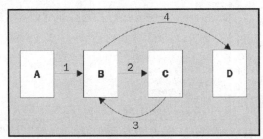

Potential order of page views that wouldn't be tracked by server log analysis

A web server log or a network sniffing tool would not record the fact that the user ever went from *Page C* to *Page B* (because *Page B* becomes cached after the first viewing), and would mistakenly report that the user got to *Page D* from *Page C*.

However, a system based on JavaScript would report correctly that the user got to *Page D* from *Page B*.It is possible to set up a server to instruct clients not to cache pages, but the resulting performance penalty would not only be costly to the web site in terms of additional server hardware, but also cause a slower user experience for users with low-bandwidth connections.

Another reason we liked the JavaScript approach is that it distinguishes between real user behavior versus robot activity. *eBay* is a site that is targeted by many Internet robots and spiders. Because JavaScript typically runs only in real browsers, the JavaScript approach ensures that our reports do not get tainted with inhuman, robot-like behavior, and includes only real human behavior. Another interesting side effect is that by comparing page view numbers reported by our web server logs and our JavaScript-powered web traffic analysis system, we can roughly estimate the number of page views of the site generated by robots.

A Java applet approach would also have worked for us, but Java applets have more overhead, are less compatible (the Java runtime environment is not included in the default installation of the newest versions of Internet Explorer and Windows), and we did not need Java's ability to monitor the typing behavior of our users.

How the System Works

In this section, I will describe how we implemented the SiteCatalyst tool into our site, including how we customized the service to our needs.

JavaScript, Cookies, and Web Bugs

The SiteCatalyst service has two main components: a client-side piece that uses JavaScript, cookies, and web bugs, and a server-side piece that maintains the web traffic analysis database, provides reporting capabilities, and manages access control for end users. The folks at Omniture maintain the server-side piece, so I will not describe that piece in detail. We customized the client-side code, and this is the piece that most web sites like *eBay* will need to touch the most.

The client-side piece is simple – we place a piece of JavaScript code on every page of the *eBay* site. The JavaScript code represents the brains of the client-side piece, and has three main purposes – it implements the random sampling algorithm that I'll describe in the next section, it reads and writes cookies to determine if a visitor is a repeat visitor or a new visitor, it packages the page name, page property values, unique visitor data, and technographic data into a long string, and finally inserts a web bug into the page that triggers the tracking of the page.

5

The name of the web bug is a concatenation of the long string, with .gif added to the end, and the src property of the bug's <img> tag points to a domain owned by Omniture. For instance, the following might be a snippet of JavaScript code that packages the data into a long string and emits it as a web bug.

```
<script language="JavaScript">
  imageName = "http://xxx.xxx.xxx.xxx/webbugs/" + pageName + prop1 +
prop2 + prop3 + prop4 + prop5 + technographic + visitor + ".gif";
  document.writeln("<img src=" + imageName + ">");
</script>
```

When a user visits a page of the *eBay* web site, the JavaScript code automatically runs, determines whether or not the user is in the random sample, and if so inserts the web bug into the page. In turn, the user's browser will make a request to the web bug that is hosted on the Omniture-owned domain. Finally, Omniture's server-side code parses the name of the .gif and appropriately stores the action in the web traffic analysis database.

Random Sampling

we found it cost-prohibitive to track every single page view from every single eBay user. Instead, we implemented a random sampling algorithm that tracks only one out of every 100 users to the eBay site.

Notice that as a consequence of the client-side JavaScript methodology described in the previous section, each time *eBay* receives a page view, a hit is also made to Omniture's servers. Recall that *eBay* users generate over 10 billion page views per month to the *eBay* site. Because of this, we found it cost-prohibitive to track every single page view from every single *eBay* user. Instead, we implemented a random sampling algorithm that tracks only one out of every 100 users to the *eBay* site.

We implemented random sampling in the following way. Whenever an eBay user visits a page of the *eBay* site, we check to see if that user has a special cookie (let us call it the sample cookie). If they do not, we generate a large random number and place that number persistently into the user's sample cookie. On subsequent visits, we read the value of the sample cookie, check to see if the modulus is 0 when divided by 100, and if it is, we consider that user as part of the 1% that is to be sampled. Note that unless a user deletes their cookies, their first visit to *eBay* will determine whether or not they are in the sample forever. However, because the algorithm is so simple, we can easily choose a different 1% of the user community to be in the sample, by simply changing the algorithm in the JavaScript code so the sampled modulus is something other than 0.

```
<script language="JavaScript">
  sample = ReadCookie("sample");
  if (sample % 100 == 0) {
    // user is in the sample
  } else {
    // user is not in the sample
  }
</script>
```

It is important to note that the most obvious way to do 1/100 sampling would have been to record only 1/100 of the page views that are generated, rather than using a cookie to track one in every 100 users. However, this would have rendered the page flow reports completely useless, as they would not represent real contiguous paths taken by real users. We were comfortable with using cookies for implementing sampling, as the eBay site already relies on cookies for allowing users to log in. One downside of using this approach, however, is that we cannot track users whose browsers have been set to reject cookies. Because of this, both the JavaScript and cookie acceptance technographic reports are not informative, because by definition, they will report that all users in our sample accept both JavaScript and cookies.

Respecting Users' Privacy

eBay respects users' privacy, and we make sure that any data we record in our web traffic analysis system is not personally-identifiable. The values in the sample cookies are randomly generated, and the JavaScript code that packages the data together does not send any data through the web bug that can uniquely identify the tracked user. On top of all that, recall that a given user has only a 1% chance of being tracked in the web traffic analysis system in the first place.

"Long Distance" Tracking

A major addition we made to Omniture's standard JavaScript code is something we called long-distance tracking. Recall that with the page flow reports, we can, for any given page, get a percentage breakdown of the pages immediately preceding that page, and likewise for pages immediately following that page. While this is sufficient for most situations, there were some cases where we needed to find out whether or not a particular page was viewed anywhere in the user's navigation path prior to a given page.

It is probably easiest to explain long-distance tracking by giving a concrete example. As you know, one of the most encouraged activities on the site is bidding, because the more bids placed, the more vibrant the marketplace is. But before users can bid on items, they need to find them. *eBay* provides a number of ways for potential buyers to find interesting items – four of the most popular finding methods are through features called "*search*," "*browse*," "*my eBay*", and "*seller's other items*." We wanted to know how many bids come from each of those methods.

Someone unfamiliar with the *eBay* site might suggest that we simply look at the "*previous page*" report for the bid confirmation page, a page called *AcceptBid*. However, users cannot arrive at the *AcceptBid* page directly from the *Search*, *Browse*, *MyeBay*, and *SellersOtherItems* pages. Instead, all users must go through the *MakeBid* page first, which is an intermediate preview page that users see to verify their bid amounts. Therefore, the "previous page" report for the *AcceptBid* page is quite uninformative, as it lists only a single page – the *MakeBid* page. The following figure shows a typical sequence of pages that a user goes through to bid on an item:

5

eBay

Search (drops LastList cookie)

ViewItem

MakeBid

AcceptBid

The solution to this problem was to drop a cookie whenever a user views a *Search*, *Browse*, *MyeBay*, or *SellersOtherItems* page. We overwrite this cookie even if the cookie already exists. We called this cookie the `LastList` cookie, because it always contains the page name of the last page that contained a list of items. Then, whenever a user arrives at the *AcceptBid* page, the JavaScript code sets one of the page property values to the value of the `LastList` cookie. Finally, we can simply look at the report for that particular page property to get a count of how many bids came from each of the four main finding methods.

Typical route through the site. The eBay™ Mark is a trademark of eBay™ Inc. eBay™ screenshots used by permission of eBay™ Inc.

Note that we had to write special JavaScript code to implement long-distance tracking. A more general approach would be to have a "previous page" report that could look further back into a user's navigation path without the use of explicit cookies. This requires more data storage, but at the time of writing, Omniture was still testing this feature.

How Page Names and Page Properties Are Set

Recall that the JavaScript code is responsible for packaging the page name and page properties (along with unique visitor and technographic data) together and setting the name of the web bug appropriately. However, it does not set the names of the pages. The names of the pages are set in two ways. For static HTML pages, the JavaScript simply uses the HTML page title (whatever is within the *<title>* tag) as the page name. For dynamic pages generated by ISAPI or J2EE, the C++ or Java code actually emits a small JavaScript variable onto the page with the name of that page, which is either the ISAPI function name for that page, or the Java servlet function name.

```
<script language="JavaScript">
  var pageName = "PageViewItem";
</script>
```

The reason that we do not use the HTML page title as the page name for dynamic pages is that the HTML page titles often already have item numbers and user IDs in them, which would make our page names much too granular (recall the discussion earlier about ViewItem and how we did not want to track each individual item's ViewItem separately).

We set page properties in a similar way. We do not use page properties for static pages, and only a small handful of dynamic pages use page properties. The ISAPI or J2EE code simply emits JavaScript variables specific to the particular page:

```
<script Language="JavaScript">
  var region = ""
  var category0 = "99"
  var category1 = "26395"
  var category2 = "11775"
  var category3 = "11781"
  var category4 = ""
  var itemPrice = "3"
  var itemTimeElasped = "8"
  var itemTimeRemaining = "10"
  var itemNumBids = "7"
</script>
```

In this example, notice that we actually track an item's entire category hierarchy, and use category numbers rather than category names. Also, for properties such as `itemTimeElapsed` and `itemTimeRemaining`, rather than recording the actual time left, we group times in buckets and report time buckets instead. For instance, bucket 10 for `itemTimeRemaining` means that there are over 6 days remaining in the auction when this page was viewed. Bucket 9 would translate to between five and six days remaining.

Another feature we added to our client-side code was the ability to change the page name on the fly. Again, an example might best explain this feature. The *eBay* homepage contains hundreds of links, and because it receives millions of page views a day, we want to measure how often users actually click on those links. The most obvious report to use for this is the "next page" report, which shows a breakdown of what pages users go to immediately after the homepage. This report works well in most cases, but in cases where the homepage includes more than one link to the same destination, the "next page" report cannot distinguish between clicks to those links – regardless of which of the links a user clicks, the "next page" report will record it as the same page. For instance, in the following figure, the "*eBay Motors*" and "*Cars, Trucks, Parts*" links bring users to the exact same page, namely a page named *eBay* Motors:Home.

In order to track clicks to those links independently, we implemented a general method for overriding a page name on the fly. By simply adding an `ssPageName` parameter to any link on the *eBay* site, as in:

http://pages.eBay.com/eBaymotors/index.html?ssPageName=ML01
or
http://pages.eBay.com/eBaymotors/index.html?ssPageName=MOPS5:HML02

Both links take you to the same page. The eBay™ Mark is a trademark of eBay™ Inc. eBay™ screenshots used by permission of eBay™ Inc.

we can append any string (in this case, *ML01* or *MOPS5:HML02*) to the subsequent page's page name. So when users click on one of the links above, the page name as recorded in the web traffic analysis system becomes *eBay Motors:Home:ML01* or *Motors:Home:MOPS5:HML02*, depending on which link the user clicked. The *ssPageName* parameter is recognized only by the JavaScript code, and is otherwise ignored by *eBay's* application server.

Putting It to Real Use

Now that we have the basics in place, let us walk through two detailed examples that illustrate how we took advantage of our web traffic analysis system. In the first example, I show how we used the tools described above to determine whether or not a major change to the selling flow actually made a positive difference to the completion rate for selling. In the second example, I discuss how we used the tools to analyze how well our finding methods assisted users to find items on which to bid.

Selling Flow

The selling flow is the sequence of pages that a seller goes through in order to list an item for sale. Several years ago it began as a short, simple sequence of pages: a page for selecting a main category, an item entry form for entering the title, description, category, and starting price, a verification page allowing the users to proofread their entries and review the fees, and finally a confirmation page to congratulate the user on having successfully listed an item. However, over time, as we added new features to eBay, the item entry form grew to be quite long, and we became worried that sellers were not completing the process due to the sheer length of the form.

The Old Flow Versus the New Flow

Therefore, we embarked on a project to convert the selling flow to one that consisted of more, but shorter pages. In the new flow, the number of pages to get through the selling flow would be higher, but each page would be more easily digestible by the sellers.

The figure below shows the old sequence of pages:

eBaySellItem

ListItemsForSale

The old way through the site. The eBay™ Mark is a trademark of eBay™ Inc. eBay™ screenshots used by permission of eBay™ Inc.

VerifyNewItem

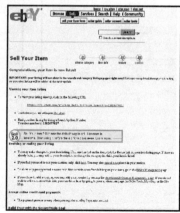

AddNewItem

eBay

5

Below is the new sequence of pages:

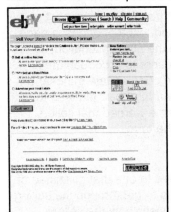

SYI_Format

SYI_CatMeta

SYI_CatLeaf

SYI_Title

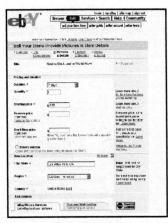

SYI_Details

The new way through the site. The eBay™ Mark is a trademark of eBay™ Inc. eBay™ screenshots used by permission of eBay™ Inc.

SYI_Payments

SYI_Verify

SYI_Confirm

The Analysis

The goal of the redesign was to increase the completion rate for the selling flow. We defined the completion rate to be the rate at which sellers successfully list an item for sale after embarking on the process. Though we usability-tested the new selling flow with a handful of real users and received encouraging results, we wanted to see how the new flow fared in the real world with millions of users.

The simplest way to compute the completion rate would be to take the number of page views of the confirmation page (*AddNewItem* in the old flow and *SYI_Confirm* in the new flow) as the numerator, and take number of page views of the starting page (*eBaySellItem* in the old flow and *SYI_Format* of the new flow) as the denominator. However, this method is inaccurate, because it assumes that the first page always represents the start of the process, that no other page can represent the start of the process, and that the last page always signifies the successful end of the process. Let us look at the simpler, old flow to see why these assumptions are false.

The first two pages of the old selling flow are shown here:

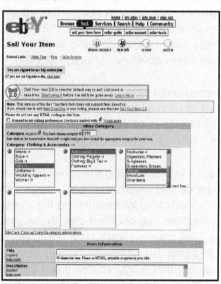

The first stages of the old route. The eBay™ Mark is a trademark of eBay™ Inc. eBay™ screenshots used by permission of eBay™ Inc.

In the old flow, the most common way for sellers to begin the selling process was to click on the *Sell* button in the *eBay* navigation bar at the top of every page, which would bring them to *eBaySellItem*. On this page, sellers chose a top-level category and were then brought to the *ListItemForSale*, which displayed the form for choosing a subcategory, entering the title and description for the item, providing detailed information about the item, and setting the payment options. There are three reasons that simply using the page view count of *eBaySellItem* as the denominator is flawed:

- Though most users indeed begin the selling process by clicking on the *Sell* button in the navigation bar, another common way for sellers to begin the process is to click on a "*Sell Your Item in this Category*" link within the browse pages, which bring sellers directly to the *ListItemForSale* page, thereby bypassing the *eBaySellItem* page altogether.

- The page view count for *eBaySellItem* includes not only page views in which a seller clicks on the *Sell* button, but also page views in which the seller uses the browser's back button from the *ListItemForSale* page after changing her mind about the top-level category. We know anecdotally that many high-volume sellers will, after having finished the listing of an item, click on the browser back button twice from the *AddNewItem* page to begin the listing of a similar item in the same category as the previous item. This technique allows savvy sellers to reuse field entries from a just-listed item for the listing of a new item. However, this also represents yet another case in which a seller bypasses the *eBaySellItem* page in listing an item.

Similarly, simply using the page view count of *AddNewItem* as the numerator in the completion rate formula is also flawed. We know that many sellers, just after successfully listing an item, will click on the link to view their *ViewItem* page for their item listing, then click the back button, causing another *AddNewItem* page view. However, this second *AddNewItem* obviously should not be counted as a successfully listed item.

OK, so enough about the problems with using simple page views to calculate completion rates. Let us now talk about how we used more sophisticated web traffic analysis techniques to overcome these problems, and created a more accurate estimate of the completion rate for the old selling flow.

The trick to overcoming the flaws listed above was to use "previous page" reporting to help us decide whether or not a page view should be counted as part of the calculation. More specifically, for calculating the denominator, rather than counting all page views to *eBaySellItem*, we counted only those that did not have *ListItemForSale* as its previous page. This way, we were sure not to accidentally count instances in which the seller was simply using the browser's back button to change an item's category. Then, to make up for the fact that many sellers enter the selling flow by clicking on the "*Sell Your Item in this category*" link from the browse pages, and therefore bypass the eBaySellItem page, we added all page views of *ListItemForSale* that came from the browse pages to the denominator, but of course did not count those that came simply from *eBaySellItem*.

Adjusting the numerator in the calculation was equally simple. Rather than counting all page views to *AddNewItem*, we counted only those page views that came from *VerifyNewItem*. This way, we were sure not to double-count *AddNewItem* page views that came from a seller clicking the browser's back button.

Calculating the completion rate for the new selling flow was similar. Rather than relying on raw page views, we looked at "previous page" reports to decide whether or not a page view should be counted. As in the old flow, there are multiple ways to initiate the selling process. In fact the new flow actually encourages users to bypass certain pages to make listing multiple, similar items, a quick process. For instance, as shown in the following screenshot, the new flow makes it possible for users to click buttons labeled "*Sell a Similar Item*" and "*Sell a Different Item*," which bring sellers to the *SYI_CatLeaf* and *SYI_Format* pages, respectively.

The confirm your sale page. The eBay™ Mark is a trademark of eBay™ Inc. eBay™ screenshots used by permission of eBay™ Inc.

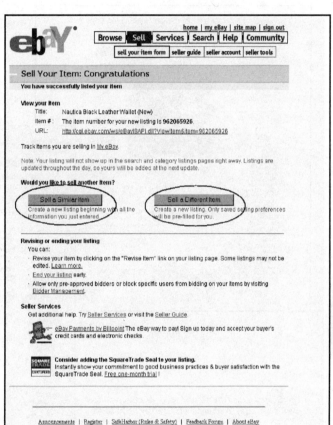

Therefore, just as with the old flow, to calculate the denominator correctly for the new selling flow, we had to use "previous page" reporting to take into account how sellers got to the *SYI_CatLeaf* and *SYI_Format* pages to decide whether or not they should count.

So how did the new selling flow fare? In the end, we were pleased to learn that the new selling flow improved the completion rate of the selling process from 60% to 75% — well worth the development effort!

Bidding Analysis

While selling is an integral piece of the eBay marketplace, we learned early on at eBay that an active buying and bidding community is what really ignites a marketplace. Therefore, as we discussed briefly before, we provide multiple ways for prospective buyers to find items in which they are interested. Four of the most popular ways are "*Search*," "*Browse*," "*my eBay*", and "*seller's other items*."

The Four Finding Methods

Search is the most frequently used finding method, and provides users with the ability to search for items with specific words in their titles and descriptions. We display a search box prominently on the *eBay* homepage so that users can begin their searching experience immediately. Once a user types a keyword and clicks the "*Find It*" button, they are brought to the search results page, which is named *Search*, as shown in the following figure:

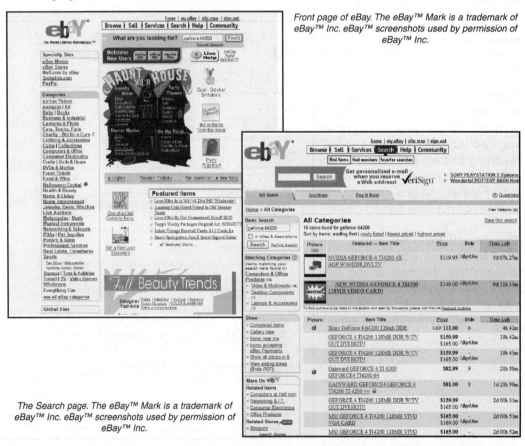

Front page of eBay. The eBay™ Mark is a trademark of eBay™ Inc. eBay™ screenshots used by permission of eBay™ Inc.

The Search page. The eBay™ Mark is a trademark of eBay™ Inc. eBay™ screenshots used by permission of eBay™ Inc.

The **Browse** option allows buyers to find items by looking through item listings per category. While search is useful when buyers know exactly what they are looking for (say, "Geforce Ti4200"), browsing is more appropriate when a buyer merely wants to "window-shop" in a particular category of goods (LCD/Flat Panel monitors, for instance). The browse pages are arranged hierarchically by category, and are named *Browse*. Examples of two browse pages are shown opposite.

Browse

Browse deeper subcategory

Browse and more detailed browse. The eBay™ Mark is a trademark of eBay™ Inc. eBay™ screenshots used by permission of eBay™ Inc.

My eBay is a feature that keeps track of all the items that a particular user has either bid on or has book-marked using *eBay's* item watching feature. Users often come here to find items in which they have previously expressed interest. There are several pages in the My *eBay* section, each represented by a tab at the top, but the page of interest and the one shown here is the *MyeBayBidding* page:

MyeBay bidding page. The eBay™ Mark is a trademark of eBay™ Inc. eBay™ screenshots used by permission of eBay™ Inc.

Finally, the **seller's other items** feature allows buyers to see a list of all items offered by a particular seller. The most common way for buyers to get to this page is to click on the view seller's other items link on the *ViewItem* page. The page that shows a seller's list of items is named *SellersOtherItems*:

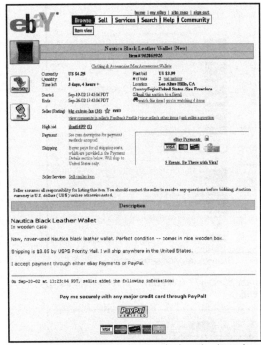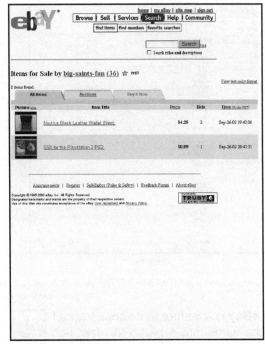

Moving from viewing one item, to viewing other items from the same seller. The eBay™ Mark is a trademark of eBay™ Inc. eBay™ screenshots used by permission of eBay™ Inc.

The Goal

The goal of this analysis was to find out how effective each of the four finding methods is in getting prospective buyers to bid. We defined effectiveness in three ways:

- **Productivity**. This is simply the percentage of total bids that come from a particular finding method. If we managed a chain of brick-and-mortar shoe stores, then a productivity report would simply show, in percentages, a breakdown of how much each store contributed in total unit sales. For *eBay*, each of our four finding methods is like a different shoe store.

- **Efficiency**. This is the number of items that a buyer views on average when using a particular finding method before finally bidding. For a shoe store, this would be the number of shoes a typical shopper tries on before buying a pair of shoes.

- **Conversion Rate**. This is a measure of how likely a buyer is to bid in a given finding session. To continue with the shoe store analogy, this would be the probability that a shopper buys a pair of shoes after walking into the store, regardless of how many shoes the shopper tries on.

While each of the three measurements is related to one other (a better efficiency should result in a higher conversion rate), they each measure a different aspect of effectiveness, and having all three measurements can help your decision-making. For instance, just because a particular shoe outlet sells the most shoes and therefore has the highest productivity, it might actually have poor salespeople and exhibit a low conversion rate. In the meantime, you might have a different shoe store in a less-trafficked part of town that might have a low productivity but high conversion rate. In such a scenario, you might be well served to transfer your better salespeople from the lower volume store to the higher volume store, or devote more advertising dollars to the less-trafficked store. In *eBay's* case, this would be analogous to driving more click-throughs to finding methods with higher conversion rates, and decreasing promotion for those finding methods that are less likely to drive bidding.

Our Analysis

Productivity was by far the easiest measurement to calculate. As discussed earlier, we implemented long-distance tracking that could tell us how many bids came from each of the finding methods. Converting the absolute numbers to percentages is obviously straightforward, and we found that *Search* was the most productive of the finding methods, and *Browse* was the least productive.

Efficiency was a tad harder to calculate, but still not difficult. Recall that we defined efficiency to be the average number of items that a buyer views before finally placing a bid. Therefore, we first used a previous page report for *ViewItem* to come up with the numerators for each of the finding methods. The previous page report tells us the number of page views to *ViewItem* that each of the finding methods generates. Then, the denominator for each of the finding methods is simply the absolute number of bids that each finding method generates. For *Search*, the calculation was:

$$\frac{\text{ViewItem page views from Search}}{\text{AcceptBid page view from Search}}$$

We found that *MyeBayBidding* was the most efficient of the finding methods, and that *Browse* was the least efficient. This makes sense, since *MyeBayBidding* displays items in which we already know that buyers have expressed interest, while Browse shows a very broad list of items based merely on a category.

Conversion Rate was the most difficult to calculate, because it requires the notion of a finding session. We defined conversion rate to be the likelihood that a user would bid in a session, so we first had to find a simple way to use web traffic analysis to calculate how many sessions of each finding method we get. Let us take *Search* as our example. When users type in a keyword on the homepage and hit "*Find It*," we consider that the beginning of a search session.

However, once the search results are shown, if a user then clicks on a different page number, or drills into a more specific category, we consider that activity part of the same session, despite the fact that our web traffic analysis system will report those as additional page views for *Search*. Likewise, if a user clicks on an item from the search results page, then clicks the browser's back button to return to the search results page, we do not count the additional *Search* page view as a new session, but rather a part of the current session. Therefore, we calculate sessions by counting only those *Search* page views whose previous page was neither *Search* itself, nor *ViewItem*. That number became our denominator, and we used the absolute number of bids from Search as our numerator.

We found that even though Search is our most productive finding method, it only ranked third in conversion rate. On the other hand, *SellersOtherItems* exhibited a high conversion rate and a low productivity, telling us that the *SellersOtherItems* is under-utilized. We immediately embarked on a project to make more visible the link to *SellersOtherItems*, to drive more traffic to that feature. Once that is in place, we plan to see if *SellersOtherItems* can still maintain its high conversion rate.

$$\frac{\textbf{AcceptBid} \text{ page views from } \textbf{Search}}{\textbf{Search} \text{ page views not from } \textbf{Search} \text{ itself or } \textbf{ViewItem}}$$

Summary

In this chapter, we gave an introduction to *eBay*, its business model, and its high-level needs for a web traffic analysis system. We then outlined our specific requirements for a web traffic analysis system, which included:

- Page View Reports, which display the number of page views each unique page at eBay receives.

- Unique Visitor Reports, which give an estimate of the number of unique visitors to each *eBay* subsite, and to *eBay* as a whole.

- Page Flow Analysis, which allows us to determine for any given page how users got to that page, and where they went afterwards.

- Technographic Reports, which show information such as browser types and screen sizes.

- Page Property Reports, which allow us to get further details about page views to the most highly visited pages of the site.

We also learned how *eBay* tailored the client-side piece of a web traffic analysis system to include random sampling, long-distance tracking, and page name changing on the fly.

We finished off by demonstrating how we used our web traffic analysis system to learn about two of the most important features of *eBay*: selling and bidding. We took you through an analysis of the completion rate of an old selling flow versus a new selling flow, and showed how we assessed the effectiveness of four different finding methods on the *eBay* site.

5

eBay

6

- Changing site, changing analysis demands
- Analysis driving site and business changes
- Tracking different types of user

Author: Ben Pearce

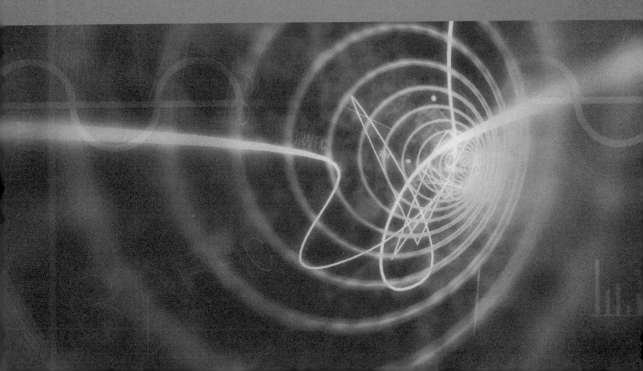

ASPToday

Ben joined Wrox Press in Birmingham, UK, as an analyst in Summer 2000, and has spent a large proportion of his time working with the 'Direct' team, the owners of Wrox's customer facing web sites, including Wrox.com, Wroxbase (books online), and its Journal sites. Much of his work has involved aiding business decisions based on his analysis of customer online activity and purchasing patterns, supporting and influencing editorial decisions and generally circulating standard (and occasionally non-standard!) web analysis to the business.

In June 2002, Ben took over business responsibility for Wrox's daily journal web site ASPToday and its sister site C#Today. In this role he is continuing to use web analytics to influence marketing strategies and editorial direction in conjunction with the site editors, with the goals of raising the profile of the sites, increasing subscription levels, and improving customer retention. These goals are achieved by looking to ensure the content and services provided best suit the customers' needs as professional programmers. Ben can be contacted at ben@asptoday.com.

Content and Visitor Profile

Since February 1999, *ASPToday* (*http://www.ASPToday.com/*) from Wrox Press has been publishing a new article every working day. The site's audience is composed of professional programmers working with Microsoft's web development technologies, including ASP versions 2, 3, and ASP.NET, SQL Server, Visual Basic, and, most recently, C#.

The current version of the site offers various subscription packages giving access to the archive of over one thousand articles, each of between 2000 and 5000 words, alongside free articles, reference material, tips, news, and PDF downloads. *ASPToday* has over 140,000 unique e-mail registrants and a significant paying subscriber base.

In this case study we will follow the growth of traffic analysis on the site, from the early days when the site was small and the analysis was simplistic, to the current subscription site, with detailed and reliable data-mining techniques. We will examine the specific business requirements that emerged as the site grew, and the issues raised by the redesigns, both aesthetic and architectural. Finally, we cover in detail several ways in which the custom-built traffic analysis system can help the business develop, and offer better and more targeted content and subscription packages to the readers.

History and Background

ASPToday was launched in February 1999, with an ambitious brief to publish a new article every working day. The site was completely free and had a fairly basic structure, designed to test the market for such a content-intensive site. After a few months, the potential for *ASPToday* was very evident, with over ten thousand registrations for the e-mail newsletter.

The original 100% Free ASPToday Logo (1999)

In October 1999 we launched the second version of the site, building on the experience of the first version. We knew at this stage that the content we were offering was popular, but the design of the site needed updating, with improved features for the readers, and a potential revenue stream: advertising. The result was more ambitious, with improved content search functionality, article ratings, and user forums. Version two saw the ability to host sponsor advertisements, both as standard banners and buttons on the site itself, and as text inserts in the weekly and daily newsletters.

Traffic and registrations continued to grow, and *ASPToday* established itself as a leading free resource for professional programmers. The demand for the site was so great that within a year of the second version going live, it was apparent that a considerable investment in rebuilding the site, and hosting it on a more scalable architecture would be required. The development costs of this rebuild, coupled with the fact that every article was written and reviewed by paid professional programmers and edited by the full-time editorial team, required a new, and again more ambitious, business model.

January 2001 saw the launch of version three, which introduced a subscription model for the growing archive of over 500 articles, whilst keeping the daily article free for 48 hours after publication. Though something of a shot in the dark, the new subscription version of the site was a great success, with thousands of readers signing up at the introductory rate of US$30 for complete access to the archive for twelve months.

This version of the site looked something like this:

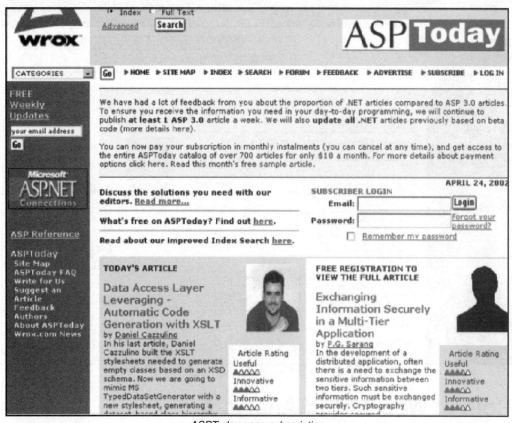

ASPToday goes subscription

After the introductory period, the annual price was set at $99, but it soon emerged that more fine-grained subscription packages were required (and we look into these developments later in this study). The system was refined in order to offer access on a monthly or quarterly basis, and access to discrete sections of the archive, as well as sales of individual PDF downloads of the articles. Between January 2001 and August 2002 the site evolved on an incremental basis, adding the packages mentioned above, but also improving the business logic "middle-tier" of the implementation, giving it more efficient and scalable performance.

The fourth and current version of the site was launched in August 2002, which saw a cleaner and more user-friendly interface, as well as additional functionality such as more advanced search options, book-marking, and printer-friendly options. *ASPToday* is now the product of almost four years experience of developing a dynamic and evolving site that offers regular high-quality articles, and a variety of subscription packages.

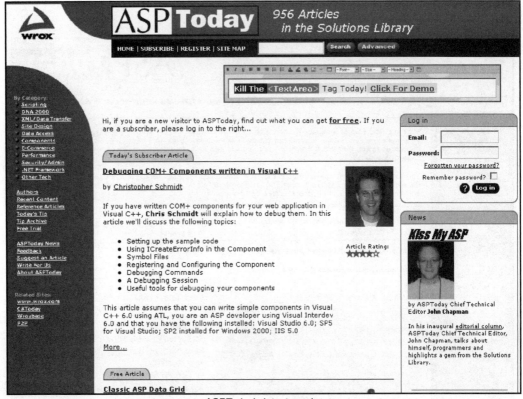

ASPToday's latest version

Role of Web Traffic Analysis

Web traffic analysis has been a crucial component in the development of *ASPToday* since its inception. It is more important now than ever, as the site depends upon accurate intelligence to inform the key business decisions that have influenced its evolution from a simple static web site to a dynamic e-commerce application. Historically, the site has relied upon two distinct sources of information on visitor activity: registration for e-mail newsletters (and, of course, paying subscriptions), and "traditional" analysis of page impressions.

Before the launch of the subscription site in 2001, the task of establishing accurate data on visitor activity was extremely difficult, and fraught with inconsistent and obscure information. The key metrics were page impressions and unique visitors. Most of the analysis was conducted using standard "out-of-the-box" log file analysis tools, although we were able to conduct some analysis of unique visitors using our own cookie-setting code. It is informative to examine briefly the problems experienced with using these two techniques.

Problems with Early Log Analysis

During the early development of *ASPToday*, the business team relied on various standard log analysis packages, but soon encountered problems when trying to interpret the reports that were generated. As we did not have direct access to the data behind the numbers that the tools were displaying, only the final generated report, we were frustrated by our inability to build more finely detailed customized output. We found that the problem with "user-friendly" tools that try to hide their functionality (or allow the user to ignore it) is that, as web traffic analysis is so context sensitive, not knowing exactly where a number came from renders it close to meaningless. Clarity and visibility would be essential for future web traffic analysis implementations.

> *page impressions, though an important metric, are more slippery to pin down than is often assumed*

It soon became apparent that page impressions, though an important metric, are more slippery to pin down than is often assumed. For example, with better site navigation and searching, a user might generate fewer page impressions to get to the desired content. This is a "good thing", but simply counting the page impressions will not help, as the navigation changed from one site to the next, and we could not therefore compare the two sets of numbers. This discovery, coupled with the standard problems of gathering reliable data in the first place, framed our difficulties with web traffic analysis in the early development of *ASPToday*.

It was not at all clear how the system had generated the figures, so we gradually began to loose faith in them (for example, we did not know whether robot traffic had been removed from the data, and if it had, how up-to-date the list of known robots used was). At the time, due to that lack of technical input into the web traffic analysis, we did not fully appreciate or measure the influence of robots. We knew the numbers might not be trustworthy, but didn't know how, or to what extent.

These tools would typically present log data in the form of attractive charts, and would be fairly useful when detailing such factors as the distribution of activity throughout the day or week. Those of us doing the analysis were not involved directly in the technical implementation of the site, and the way the statistical analysis was generated was not clear. It was essentially this problem that persuaded us that we needed to have more control and accountability for the numbers.

A separate problem, aside from the difficulty in interpreting the reported results, was introduced by moving from one version of the site to the next. With the development of version two, which introduced advertising onto the site for the first time, it was important to predict how many page impressions we would be generating, in order to plan the potential advertising inventory available. Because the site was being completely overhauled, however, it was not possible to predict how user behavior would be translated onto the new format, with improved search facilities and navigation, and additional features such as discussion forums.

Learning from these early experiences of log analysis, when the time came to build the next version of the site (version three discussed in detail below), the technical and business teams worked together to determine what information was required, and the new system was built in-house. We decided to "build" rather than "buy" because it gave us exactly what the business needed and ensured that there was always an explanation for the generation of the numbers.

Cookie Data Analysis

Using the data we gathered from cookies was a little easier, but it presented its own unique challenges. Visitors to the site were sent a cookie in the HTTP response. The cookie, set to expire after three months, included a Globally Unique ID (GUID), and was created by a small Visual Basic component. The component would then check for cookie data in the incoming requests, and record the GUIDs in a database. Querying that data was useful for giving us a rough-and-ready indication as to the number of unique visitors in a given period of time.

The drawback of such a system was the inaccuracy implicit in the cookie system. Firstly, we estimated that a possibly significant number of visitors were browsing with the "accept cookies" option turned off in their browser. Secondly we would be effectively "double-counting" those visitors who used more than one machine (or browser) – for example one at home and one at the office – which could be fairly significant for our Internet-aware readership. While this would in part be mitigated by those users who might share a machine, this behavior would probably be relatively rare. Crucially, accurate numbers for both of these types of user would be impossible to determine. It is worth considering that the extent of this problem will differ depending on the audience for the site: a technical audience such as ours is more likely to run different machines, and separate browsers on those machines, than a more general site.

With the development of the subscription version of the site, the opportunity arose to develop a more accurate system for data gathering and analysis. The old problem of cross-site comparability occurred again of course, as the move to subscription meant that we would inevitably experience a drop in total page impressions, as the majority of pages would now only be available to paying customers. It is this new system that we will discuss in detail in the rest of the case study.

Overview of Web Hosting Architecture

The subscription version of the site was launched in January 2001. Since then, the basic features on the site have remained the same, though the underlying technical implementation has been improved significantly. For instance, the middle-tier components were rewritten in COM+, giving significant performance and scalability advantages over standard COM implementations. For the sake of clarity, when discussing the technical architecture of the system, reference will be made only to the implementation current at the end of 2002.

> COM+ is an extension to Microsoft's COM (Component Object Model). For more details, see
> *http://www.microsoft.com/com/tech/complus.asp*

ASPToday is hosted on an n-tier architecture comprised of two load-balanced Microsoft Windows 2000 Enterprise Servers running IIS, a middle tier of two COM+ servers with custom business logic components written in Visual Basic 6, and a database layer of a cluster of two copies of Microsoft SQL Server Enterprise. This architecture is highly scalable, as new servers can be slotted in to improve performance as the site traffic expands, and the system can automatically adjust if one of the servers goes down, or needs to be taken out temporarily for maintenance.

Overview of Business Logic Architecture

The analysis data is collected by the business logic component, and stored and retrieved in the SQL Server database. The component handles the session management on the site, as well as providing functionality for subscribers to log in and out, and verifying whether a request for a subscriber-only page has been made by a valid user (that is, a logged-in subscriber to the correct package). It is worth examining how the component uses the database to verify and record this information, as it is the key to the powerful analysis tools used on *ASPToday*.

The purpose of this system is twofold: firstly to facilitate a membership-based site and maintain session state, and secondly to record detailed information on the use of the site by the visitors. As a result, the business logic essentially differentiates three distinct types of users:

- **Anonymous User**

  Users who have not identified themselves to the site by logging in. This group includes those who have previously logged in but have not yet done so in this session, as well as those who have never identified themselves to us at any point. Anonymous users are exactly that: we have no way of telling who they are, until they register with us. This data is therefore similar to that which one might gather from a detailed analysis of the server log files, with all of the accompanying issues. In fact, our analysis concentrates on the paying subscribers in order to improve the service and the way it is used, so the inaccuracies of the anonymous user are not critical.

- **Member**

  A user who has identified themselves to the site by "joining" (in practice registering with us by giving us their e-mail address and a password), and then logging in for this session. Sections of the archive are available free to Members.

- **Subscriber**

  A member who has signed up for one of the paid subscriptions on the site, allowing them access to the archive of articles, or a part of it. Subscribers are a subset of members.

Session state is maintained by the use of session tokens, set by the component either in a cookie, or, if the user does not have cookies enabled, in the query string of the URL. The token is a long alphanumeric string which is composed of random elements, keys in the database to guarantee uniqueness, check digits, and the ID of the session to which it belongs. The sequence of events managed by the component is as follows:

1. A request is received by one of the IIS servers. The component checks whether there is a token sent in the request (either in the cookie data, or in the query string of the URL requested).

2. If there is no token present, the component creates a new session in the database, and then generates a unique token for that session. That token is then included in any response back to the visitor in their cookie, if appropriate, or included in all hyperlinks on the page requested – ensuring that the token is available to the component to maintain the session when the visitor clicks one of the links to continue their visit. The details of the initial request, including URL and query string data, are also recorded in the database.

3. If the request does contain a token, this is checked against the session information in the database. Firstly, we establish that it is a valid token that was previously generated by the component. If so, then the time elapsed since the last request in that session is checked, to verify that the session is not deemed to have "timed out".

An invalid token (such as one that has been tampered with, deliberately or otherwise), or a timed out session, results in a message requesting the user to log in again. If the timed out session is then successfully reactivated by a valid log in, the user is redirected to the page which was requested when they timed out. To aid usability, Members can elect to receive a cookie which "remembers" them, and ensures that they do not have to log in on each visit, and that their session does not time out. For security purposes, this cookie can be easily deactivated from the Member's preferences page. If all is well, then the details of the request are recorded and the session continues.

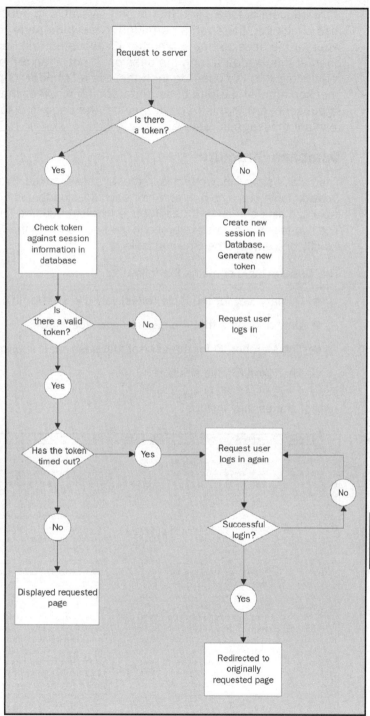

If the request is for a page that is only available to subscribers, then the system will also check that the user is permitted to view the page. The component checks whether the session has a Member ID allocated to it, indicating that the user has been authenticated during the session. If not, then a message is returned requesting that the user log in. If there is a Member ID present, then this is checked against the database to determine whether that member has access rights (a subscription) to this page: if they do, the page is displayed and, if not, the relevant message is returned.

Database Structure

The data is stored in two tables in the database, called *Session* and *Session_Page*. The *Session* table contains one entry for each session that is activated. The *Session_Page* table contains one entry for each page that is requested (similar to a standard log file). The two tables are cross-referenced, so each entry in the *Session_Page* table relates to exactly one entry in the *Session* table.

The *Session* table contains the following:

- Primary Key for the table (effectively the Session ID)
- Date and Time that the session was activated
- The Member ID for the user of that session, if applicable
- The token for this session

Typical entries may include:

	SessionID	SessionStartDate	MemberID	Token
1542	79257	2002-03-06 00:09:04.183	NULL	79257Z63YHwx3glrfhrVO7QUgL
1543	79282	2002-03-06 00:09:00.120	NULL	79282ZuKOw53PAs1wsOC86BlH1
1544	79291	2002-03-06 00:01:21.217	132360	79291ZtjK1GjPkEM1csrRvGc6m
1545	79295	2002-03-06 02:35:21.237	94506	79295ZvDDCOxspnEMaPwktvtdy
1546	79297	2002-03-06 00:08:15.793	NULL	79297Z530WCrY4tEWt8LrdueSt
1547	79299	2002-03-06 00:05:52.137	NULL	79299Z0c1KDb3AjE6dxE3L8wvS
1548	79302	2002-03-06 00:03:20.250	NULL	79302ZgvFbufSP74DhrEtmMcXJW
1549	79309	2002-03-06 00:02:31.720	132362	79309Zo6M74fyad61TVypv2EWD
1550	79316	2002-03-06 00:16:32.167	132372	79315Zts1IqahEUthE6cQVwAIG
1551	79323	2002-03-06 00:06:43.997	NULL	79323ZXRfRVGhO4cDY5vRv6FCH
1552	79341	2002-03-06 00:09:11.870	NULL	79341ZXX2rTU502sndSRu7KFrr
1553	79343	2002 03 06 00:00:55.580	28004	79343ZRR7MC3S1qFuwJu8V1K63
1554	79345	2002-03-06 00:14:43.040	132371	79345Z1FL6D1xWi3TLGUU6aEDj
1555	79347	2002-03-06 00:00:29.343	NULL	79347ZwmtAykuGjFFUt3B3bY1U
1556	79355	2002-03-06 00:09:35.700	132364	79355ZNeJEmtoU5mEUKLg1oc1d
1557	79356	2002-03-06 00:12:47.870	NULL	79356ZGLwRCydVcMWKMc40eUSJ
1558	79359	2002-03-06 00:01:03.250	50773	79359Z1E1nvfp1U3WqoVcpFfWg
1559	79361	2002-03-06 00:00:03.090	NULL	79361ZWFcbhETLEMuJyiIIxQFRM
1560	79362	2002-03-06 00:00:03.187	NULL	79362ZsvuBBigD6Ga2M1sa34LJ
1561	79363	2002-03-06 00:00:13.657	NULL	79363Z42FxS34E7rhvCWBAc2W2
1562	79364	2002-03-06 00:00:11.017	NULL	79364ZL3XxPpVJmcuDjYkJoaxW
1563	79365	2002-03-06 00:00:17.843	NULL	79365Zf5uWp34eSOTYDVe1ykJc
1564	79366	2002-03-06 00:00:17.983	NULL	79365ZyrvbWvLOBFHOSewRSVIh
1565	79367	2002-03-06 00:06:03.200	132365	79067ZkGnvA374IF1II4zw61F65
1566	79368	2002-03-06 00:00:15.500	NULL	79368ZFmeAR1Fb5EK16Go0qG1d
1567	79369	2002-03-06 00:00:21.297	NULL	79369ZN2DQPsan1cWSA5SBQHuu

The Session table

The `Session_Page` table contains the following:

- Primary Key for the table (an auto-incrementing number)
- Session ID, linking this page to the relevant entry in the Session table (Foreign Key)
- URL of the page requested
- Date and Time of the request
- Other data in the request (query string or form data, referrer, etc.)

Typical entries may include:

	ID	FK_SessionID	URL	QueryString	TimeServed	Referer
908	1084686	142381	www.asptoday.com/Default.asp	mid954	2002-03-07 05:2...	http://p2p.wrox.com/asp/
909	1083890	142266	www.asptoday.com/information/information.asp	infoid=13	2002-03-07 05:1...	http://www.asptoday.com
910	1079711	141786	www.asptoday.com/Default.asp	mid954	2002-03-07 05:0...	http://p2p.wrox.com/asp/
911	1072985	140515	www.asptoday.com/information/information.asp	infoid=13	2002-03-07 04:3...	http://www.asptoday.com/da
912	1071510	140130	www.asptoday.com/information/information.asp	infoid=9	2002-03-07 04:2...	http://www.asptoday.com/
913	1068231	139670	www.asptoday.com/information/information.asp	infoid=8	2002-03-07 04:1...	http://www.asptoday.com
914	1064642	138947	www.asptoday.com/information/information.asp	infoid=13	2002-03-07 03:5...	http://www.asptoday.com/
915	1064802	138972	www.asptoday.com/content/articles/20010712.asp	id=33	2002-03-07 03:5...	http://www.bipinjoshi.com/
916	1064807	138973	www.asptoday.com/content/articles/20010712.asp	id=33	2002-03-07 03:5...	http://www.bipinjoshi.com/
917	1052933	137298	www.asptoday.com/content/articles/20020225.asp	id=aspid0070	2002-03-07 03:1...	NULL
918	1052934	137299	www.asptoday.com/content/articles/20020225.asp	id=aspid0070	2002-03-07 03:1...	NULL
919	1051190	136764	www.asptoday.com/information/information.asp	infoid=13	2002-03-07 02:5...	http://www.asptoday.com/
920	1049405	136287	www.asptoday.com/information/information.asp	infoid=8	2002-03-07 02:4...	http://www.asptoday.com/
921	1047873	135871	www.asptoday.com/information/information.asp	infoid=8	2002-03-07 02:3...	http://www.asptoday.com/
922	1045204	135438	www.asptoday.com/Default.asp	id=aspid0070	2002-03-07 02:2...	NULL
923	1043487	135178	www.asptoday.com/Default.asp	mid126	2002-03-07 02:2...	http://activedeveloper.dk/
924	1043399	135147	www.asptoday.com/content/articles/20020225.asp	id=aspid0070	2002-03-07 02:2...	NULL
925	1043401	135148	www.asptoday.com/content/articles/20020225.asp	id=aspid0070	2002-03-07 02:2...	NULL
926	1042677	134907	www.asptoday.com/content/articles/20020225.asp	id=aspid0070	2002-03-07 02:1...	NULL
927	1042680	134909	www.asptoday.com/content/articles/20020225.asp	id=aspid0070	2002-03-07 02:1...	NULL
928	1042988	135023	www.asptoday.com/information/information.asp	infoid=13	2002-03-07 02:1...	http://www.asptoday.com/
929	1042304	134794	www.asptoday.com/information/information.asp	infoid=13	2002-03-07 02:1...	http://www.asptoday.com/
930	1042469	134835	www.asptoday.com/content/articles/20020225.asp	id=aspid0070	2002-03-07 02:1...	NULL
931	1042470	134836	www.asptoday.com/content/articles/20020225.asp	id=aspid0070	2002-03-07 02:1...	NULL
932	1041977	134706	www.asptoday.com/content/articles/20020225.asp	id=aspid0070	2002-03-07 02:1...	http://uk.f208.mail.yahoo
933	1041978	134707	www.asptoday.com/content/articles/20020225.asp	id=aspid0070	2002-03-07 02:1...	http://uk.f208.mail.yahoo
934	1042131	134748	www.asptoday.com/content/articles/20020225.asp	id=aspid0070	2002-03-07 02:1...	NULL

The Session_Page table

An offline process produces a copy of these tables every 24 hours, allowing me to query the data without affecting the performance of the live site. Also, scheduled scripts produce standard reports of key metrics (such as page impressions per new article) from the previous day. This "at a glance" information is useful for editors to get a quick overview of visitor activity. A summary of this information is mailed to the team (editorial and business) every week.

Lots of Data, Lots of Analysis

The fact that so much detail is captured and recorded in the database allows me to run very detailed queries on the data, building up a very precise picture of the usage patterns. The system is extremely powerful as an analysis tool, and some details of the sort of investigations possible will be given later. There are, however, warnings that must be given about such a system, principally relating to performance.

As the business logic component needs to connect to the database for every request, reading information and recording data, this can produce a performance bottleneck which, if not dealt with effectively, will cripple the normal operation of the site, something which is particularly undesirable when users have paid for a subscription. Since the subscription version of the site went live, we have consistently monitored and improved the architecture of the system to improve performance. The current architecture, for example, uses COM+ components in a dedicated middle tier (a set of servers whose sole purpose is to run the components) that is particularly efficient at managing database connections, the potential performance bottleneck in our system.

Example One: Regular Visitors, Frequent Viewers

As we are a site primarily funded by our readers, it is essential that we are able to offer exactly what the subscribers are looking for. To do this, we need to monitor visitor activity very closely. The detailed system that we have in place now allows us to detect the pages viewed by an individual subscriber, and consequently build up an accurate picture of how the site is being used, so we can offer more focused content and new subscription options to meet the apparent demand. We can look into how we did this in a little more detail.

I first selected a random sample of the database of subscribers, representing around 5% of the total subscriber base. I ran a simple query on the Session database that selected the total page views per day, per `MemberID` over a particular time period. In a list this data was not particularly useful, so I used Microsoft Excel to create a *PivotTable* by cross-tabulating the data, with `MemberID` along the side and the date running across the top.

The first cut summary of the data looked something like this:

Initial data summary

150

Again, in this state the data did not reveal anything particularly useful, so I conditionally formatted the cells with data in to appear shaded:

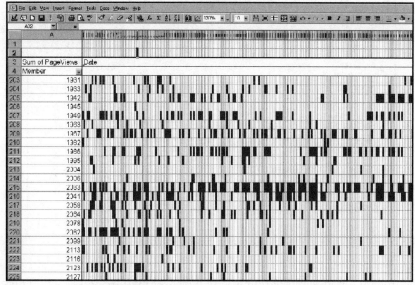

Graphical analysis techniques began to prove useful

This was developed further by adding several levels of conditional formatting based on the number of page views in each cell: the higher the number of page views in a particular day, the darker the shading of the cell. It soon became apparent that there were different categories of usage of the site. Thus I grouped the data visually into several categories ranging from 'almost never' through 'many pages on few occasions' to 'Regular heavy usage':

Almost Never:

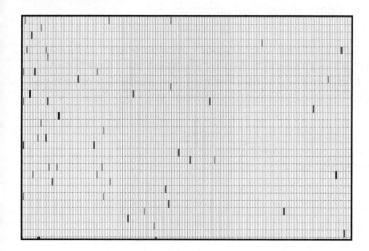

Users who rarely visit

Regular Heavy Usage:

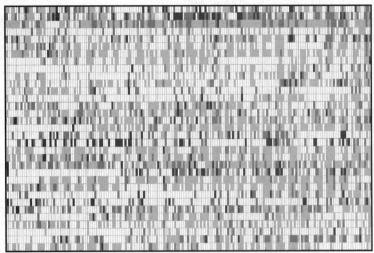

Users who visit regularly

Having determined these different patterns of activity, I then set out to categorize the entire subscriber base, based on their session data. Clearly using the above method would not have been efficient by any means, so I created rules based on the initial observations that could be integrated into SQL queries, which could be run easily against the session data. The rules consisted of metrics such as:

- Number of months which included at least one visit

- Total days in each month which included at least one visit

- Average pages viewed per visit

- Changes in the regularity of days visited, over time

This allowed me to determine the exact proportions of our customer base that belonged to each category. I later developed this method further by analyzing the difference in visiting patterns between new and seasoned subscribers, as well as looking deeper into the types of pages viewed (such as articles, reference material, etc.) over time.

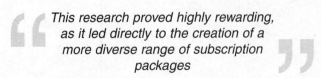

This research proved highly rewarding, as it led directly to the creation of a more diverse range of subscription packages

This research proved highly rewarding, as it led directly to the creation of a more diverse range of subscription packages targeted at actual customer needs. For example, the categorization process revealed a large subset of subscribers who seemed to use the site in sporadic but short bursts, consistent with "just-in-time" requirements. We therefore introduced a one-month "project" option, allowing users to subscribe for a lower fee, but enjoy unlimited use for the period of the subscription. We complemented this by adding the opportunity to purchase copies of single articles as PDF downloads.

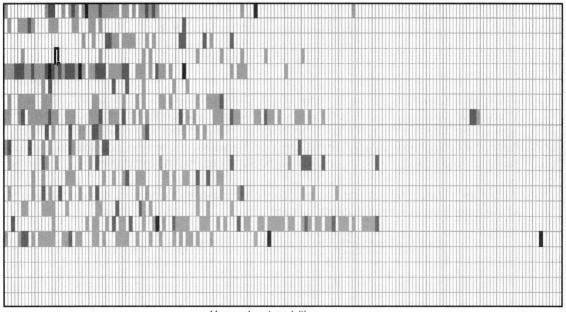

Users who stop visiting

During the process, it was also discovered that there was a subset of subscribers who seemed to visit the site fairly regularly, but then stopped suddenly.

The categorization process gave us the ability to contact these subscribers personally in order to determine their reasons for stopping visiting, and to find out if there were any features or content improvements that would make the site more useful to them.

Example Two: Topic Interest

One of the promises we make to our audience is to supply timely and relevant information on the latest technology. The introduction by Microsoft of their .NET range of software and services (at the end of 2001) presented us with a major challenge: our subscribers are professional programmers and many are therefore still actively using the previous versions of ASP, while others are starting to adopt or at least investigate ASP.NET.

> We now refer to ASP 2 and ASP 3 as "Classic ASP", to differentiate them from ASP.NET

We took an editorial decision early on to provide as much detailed and real-world information on .NET as possible, as this technology represented a major advance, and was sure to become the key area of expertise for our audience in the future. Once we had been publishing new articles about .NET for a while, it became possible to conduct research into how our subscribers were actually accessing the information.

As before, I started by running a large query on the database, producing data detailing all article pages viewed by subscriber by date:

	Member ID	URL	TimeServed
1	1568	www.asptoday.com/content/articles/19990803.asp	2002-01-05 15:37:21.040
2	1680	www.asptoday.com/content/articles/20020403.asp	2002-05-10 13:07:43.880
3	1680	www.asptoday.com/content/articles/20020403.asp	2002-05-10 13:08:04.820
4	1680	www.asptoday.com/content/articles/20020403.asp	2002-05-10 13:08:06.147
5	1680	www.asptoday.com/content/articles/20010629.asp	2002-03-13 05:07:57.117
6	1680	www.asptoday.com/content/articles/20011113.asp	2002-01-06 13:53:03.510
7	1680	www.asptoday.com/content/articles/19991022.asp	2001-11-13 15:50:17.630
8	1680	www.asptoday.com/content/articles/19990806.asp	2002-02-13 12:02:48.393
9	1680	www.asptoday.com/content/articles/19991109.asp	2002-02-13 12:01:36.817
10	1680	www.asptoday.com/content/articles/20010312.asp	2002-02-13 11:54:49.557
11	527	www.asptoday.com/content/articles/20000309.asp	2001-11-10 02:41:18.807
12	527	www.asptoday.com/content/articles/20000306.asp	2002-02-27 11:39:54.713
13	527	www.asptoday.com/content/articles/20000707.asp	2002-02-26 14:37:20.240
14	527	www.asptoday.com/content/articles/20000707.asp	2002-02-26 14:37:20.410
15	543	www.asptoday.com/content/articles/20020529.asp	2002-05-29 10:23:00.453
16	543	www.asptoday.com/content/articles/20010710.asp	2001-11-10 02:58:54.140
17	543	www.asptoday.com/content/articles/20001214.asp	2001-11-10 02:57:59.467
18	543	www.asptoday.com/content/articles/20011231.asp	2002-01-02 08:46:26.720
19	543	www.asptoday.com/content/articles/20020208.asp	2002-02-08 04:09:20.450
20	543	www.asptoday.com/content/articles/20020208.asp	2002-02-08 04:09:56.763
21	543	www.asptoday.com/content/articles/20020208.asp	2002-02-08 04:12:18.280
22	543	www.asptoday.com/content/articles/20020208.asp	2002-02-08 04:12:18.423
23	543	www.asptoday.com/content/articles/20020208.asp	2002-02-08 04:09:56.450
24	653	www.asptoday.com/content/articles/19990728.asp	2002-01-15 06:40:48.530
25	2181	www.asptoday.com/content/articles/20000518.asp	2001-11-14 13:51:08.547
26	2181	www.asptoday.com/content/articles/19990629.asp	2002-01-15 07:00:09.343
27	2353	www.asptoday.com/content/articles/20010524.asp	2002-07-30 09:06:38.770

Articles viewed by subscriber, organized by date

This data was then cross-referenced against *ASPToday*'s content database, where each article is categorized against a number of technical categories. One of these categories was '.NET' which enabled me to determine the number of .NET versus Classic articles viewed each month by each subscriber.

MemberID	ArticleType	Month	CountOfArticles
4557	Classic	Nov-01	48
4557	Classic	Dec-01	59
4557	.NET	Jan-02	2
4557	Classic	Feb-02	29
4557	.NET	Feb-02	7
4557	Classic	Mar-02	32
4557	.NET	Mar-02	8
4557	Classic	Apr-02	25
4557	.NET	Apr-02	19
4557	Classic	May-02	15
4557	.NET	May-02	26
4557	Classic	Jun-02	24
4557	.NET	Jun-02	27
4557	Classic	Jul-02	13
4557	.NET	Jul-02	26
49876	Classic	Apr-02	16
49876	.NET	Apr-02	2
49876	Classic	May-02	14
49876	.NET	May-02	5
49876	Classic	Jun-02	19
49876	.NET	Jun-02	3
49876	Classic	Jul-02	18

Subscriber article topics by month

The critical conclusion to be drawn from this analysis was that at the time *a significant proportion of our subscribers did not yet have any interest in .NET*. This result was crystallized by again applying "rules" to the data (for example, 'at least *x* Classic articles and less than *y* .NET articles viewed last month'), and examining the results.

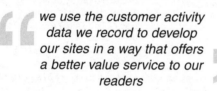

we use the customer activity data we record to develop our sites in a way that offers a better value service to our readers

Left unnoticed, this might present a major obstacle to a site that has a predominant focus on .NET technologies, and is reliant on subscribers signing up for its content. Using the analysis, however, we were able to identify a significant subset of our audience, and create a subscription package more tightly relevant to their actual needs: in this case a reduced-price subscription allowing unlimited access to the archive of just Classic articles. This also prompted us to add the ability to search just within .NET or Classic articles. This analysis therefore provides a good example of how we use the customer activity data we record to develop our sites in a way that offers a better value service to our readers, which in turn should engender a long-term subscription relationship with our customers.

Example Three: Monitoring Campaigns and Schemes

As stated earlier, the intricate nature of our traffic analysis system allows us to perform very detailed queries on the data that we collect. We took advantage of this flexibility when we decided to initiate campaigns designed to increase traffic to the site, and ultimately the number of subscriptions. Using the session management and tracking facilities that we had in place, I was able to administer and monitor both a pilot affiliate scheme and an advertising campaign on Google. To illustrate how this worked, let us look at how the affiliate scheme was organized in a little detail.

Each affiliate in the scheme was given a unique identifier which should be attached to the query string of all affiliate URLs linking to *ASPToday*. For example, if the affiliate identifier was *affid0045* and the affiliate wanted to link to the subscribe page, the URL would be *http://www.ASPToday.com/subscribe.asp?affid0045*. This is similar to other affiliate schemes that operate today. For example, the Amazon Associates scheme requires that we attach our unique identifier as part of the URLs that we use to link to Amazon, although in this case the identifier is placed in the main section of the URL, rather than in the query string.

The identifier could also be used within HTML search boxes, which could be placed on the affiliate's site so users could search *ASPToday* direct from there:

```
<table cellpadding="5" cellspacing="0" border="1" align="center">
  <td bgcolor="#CC0033" border="1" bordercolor="#CC0033"
    bordercolorlight="#000000" bordercolordark="#000000" width="70">
    <form action="http://www.asptoday.com/find.asp?affid0045" method="post"
        target="_blank">
    <font face="Verdana" color="#FFFFFF" size="3"><b>
      Search<br>
      <a href="http://www.asptoday.com/default.asp?affid0045" target="_blank">
        <font color="#FFFFFF">ASPToday</font>
      </a>
    </b></font>
    <input type="text" tabindex="1" name="q" size="12">
    <input type="image" tabindex="3" name="button"
        src="http://www.asptoday.com/ASPToday/search.gif" width="46"
        height="21" alt="Search" border="0" class="submitimage"
        align="center">
      <a href="http://www.asptoday.com/info.asp?view=SearchHelp&affid0045#FTC"
        target="_blank">
        <img src="http://www.asptoday.com/ASPToday/Images/qmark.gif"
            align="center" border="0">
      </a>
    </form>
  </td>
</table>
```

Affiliate search box

It was then possible to select from the `Session` table in the database the total clicks by date, as well as all the sessions that had been initiated with one of the affiliate scheme's unique identifiers in the query string, using queries such as:

● Clicks by date on the affiliate identifier:

```
SELECT
        CAST(CONVERT(varchar(20),TimeServed,101) As Datetime)
            As DateByDay, Count(FK_SessionID) As DailyClicks
FROM Session_Pages
WHERE QueryString Like '%affid0045%'
GROUP BY CAST(CONVERT(varchar(20),TimeServed,101) As Datetime)
```

Note: the CAST and CONVERT process simply strips off the time part of the `Datetime` field, in order to be able to group the data by day.

● Sessions initiated by a click on the affiliate identifier:

```
SELECT FK_SessionID
FROM Session_Pages
WHERE QueryString Like '%affid0045%'
GROUP BY FK_SessionID
```

Similarly, when a purchase is made on the site (see *Example Four*), various details are stored, including price paid, date, and the session ID. The session IDs for these visits could then be cross-referenced, generating a list of affiliate-initiated visits that resulted in a purchase. This enabled us to send regular reports to each of our affiliates, detailing both the total number of clicks through to *ASPToday* that they had generated, and the number and value of purchases made on these visits, and therefore the amount of affiliate income earned (a percentage of the revenue generated).

A similar method was used with a Google AdWords Select™ advertising campaign, in which each type of advertisement was given its own unique identifier. We then ran reports indicating what the response rate to these advertisements had been, and, crucially, how much revenue had been earned from purchases made from these "introductions". We were therefore able to make very accurate and invaluable ROI calculations for these advertising campaigns.

Example Four: PDF Site Analysis

Once we had introduced the option to purchase single articles as downloadable PDF files, it was important to monitor not only the sales of these documents, but also the process by which users come to purchase them. In effect, we needed to do some shopping cart analysis.

I broke the purchasing process up into a series of stages, corresponding to every page a user had to view in order to complete their purchase.

By viewing aggregated data of the number of page impressions for each page in the process, some unexpected facts emerged about the "attrition rate" from one stage to the next (the rate of decline of page impressions as the users moved through the process). The starkest discovery was that the second stage in the process had only 20% of the page impressions of the first: an attrition rate of 80% before the user had even reached the third stage of the process.

Although a certain amount of attrition is understandable, due to users entering the system out of curiosity, rather than serious purchasing intent, I concluded that the process we had in place was too laborious for the user, leading along an elaborate path which the vast majority would leave without making a purchase.

> As a result of this analysis, we simplified the shopping cart process considerably

As a result of this analysis, we simplified the shopping cart process considerably, actually halving the number of stages. In order to make the system less opaque to the user, we also included far more detail prior to stage one, allowing the user to make a more informed decision as to whether to enter the process at all. Consequently, the attrition rate dropped considerably, and overall PDF sales increased.

Example Five: Editorial Strategy

As well as informing marketing or business decisions, we have used our detailed traffic analysis to help direct and improve our editorial strategy. Monitoring the subscribers' interest in .NET as we described earlier, for example, was extremely useful to our editors, as it is a clear indication of the actual take-up rate of new technology – which is generally faster in the virtual world of computer publishing than in the real world of day-to-day requirements of professional programmers (and their employers and clients).

In practice, the business and the editorial teams on *ASPToday* work closely together, and are constantly sharing information and ideas. Take for example the analysis of the types of articles viewed by two distinct groups of users: subscribers and non-subscribers.

For individual articles in a set period as well as grouped sets of articles over time (based on a particular editorial category, for example), I calculated the proportion of views that were attributed to each group. The results were useful to our editors in demonstrating the types of article that are good for attracting new users to the site, as opposed to attending to the core interests of our paying subscribers.

more generic reports were also produced to help guide the site's editorial direction

Content that appeals to new users more than subscribers therefore is ideal for the free articles that are available on the site. As well as detailed analysis, more generic reports were also produced to help guide the site's editorial direction. For example, using a similar method as described above for the .NET vs. Classic content analysis, I regularly analyzed the proportion of views on articles split by editorial category, and the average views per article in each category, so that the editors could identify the 'hotspots' of which topics were becoming more interesting to our subscribers, as well as the 'performance' of their library of articles in general.

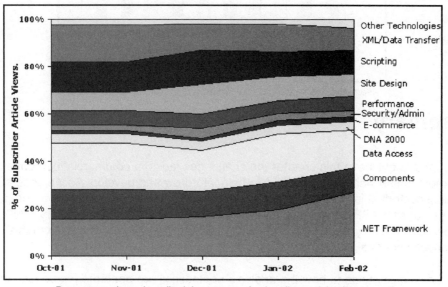

Percentage share, by editorial category, of subscriber article views over time

6

ASP Today

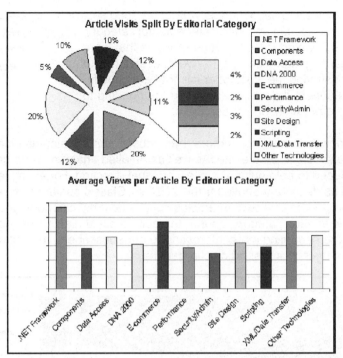

Alternative views of share by editorial category of subscriber article

Summary

I have tried to outline in this chapter the challenges facing a commercial content site as it attempts to use web traffic analysis to help it to grow and develop. As we specialize in technical content, it is important to keep on top of the needs and activities of the people that use our site. ASPToday has changed a lot since it launched in February 1999, and we now have a highly flexible and powerful data analysis system. The road to this solution was not straightforward, and lessons were learned along the way:

- Lack of clarity as to how the analysis or statistics are generated increases the difficulty of correctly interpreting the information being presented.

- Data collected in one context are more or less irrelevant in a different context, making cross-site comparison an extremely complex activity.

- Knowing your user, what they want, and how they operate, is essential to conducting meaningful web traffic analysis.

- The new system must involve more communication, and from an earlier stage, between the technical and business teams.

- Building a solution is more expensive and time-consuming than buying one in, but has the advantage that we understand the data, and can adapt our interpretation of it as the business develops.

In summary, understanding your site and its users – or customers – is the key to successful web traffic analysis. Off-the-peg analysis is rarely insightful, as there is so much diversity between different sites, business models, and web users. There is no substitute for getting to know the numbers that drive your site in intimate detail.

6

ASP Today

Index

A Guide to the Index

The index covers the numbered chapters but not the Introduction and is arranged in word-by-word order (so that, for example, New York would precede Newark). Acronyms have been preferred to their expansions as main entries as being easier to recall. Comments specifically about the index should be sent to *billj@glasshaus.com*.

B

back button use
    page flow analysis and, 117, 130
    tagging and, 13
bbbonline.org web site
    helping with misleading privacy policies, 71
    NYTimes.com web site and, 82
    privacy issues and, 66
BBC (British Broadcasting Corporation) funding
        implications, 88
    international services, 90
    reporting responsibilities and, 99
BBC News Online web site, 87-109
    archival use, 107
    example home pages
        international version, 90
        UK version, 89, 105
        World Service, 90
    overview of technical architecture, 94
    reports generated, 94-103
    requirements of traffic analysis, 94
    sample report ranking articles, 97
        international edition, 98
    September 11, 2001 effects, 106
    traffic information collected, 90
bidding analysis, eBay.com site, 131
BMRB market research company, panel surveys, 92
browser analysis as a source of traffic data, 13
browsers
    see also user agents.
    Analog browser summary report, 26
    APPEL rulesets and, 70
    P3P support, 68
browsing on categories, eBay.com site, 114, 132
business environment and analytical techniques, 37
business logic components, ASPToday.com, 145
    performance penalty, 150
buyers *see* finding methods.

C

cache-busting techniques, browser analysis, 13
caching
    circumventing using JavaScript, 120
    DNS information for Analog tool, 29
    limitations of server logs and, 10, 19
case studies in privacy
    NYTimes.com web site, 79-83
    SmartGirl.org site, 72-75
    theonion.com site, 75-79
categories of article, ASPToday.com, 155, 159, 160
categories of visitor by visit frequency, 151
children's privacy issues, 66
clear GIFs, NYTimes.com web site, 81
click-stream data, 10
    panel surveys record accurately, 11
    sever logs can't provide, 10
click-throughs
    adding to the log database, 53
    query for total clicks on a tracking link, 58
    tracking on log database, 44
client-side code
    browser analysis, 13
    use by eBay.com, 120
        page name changes, 125
COM+ (Component Object Model), 145
Comber, Pete, BBC News Online author, 87
CommerceNet Consortium, 67
communication between technical and business
teams, 160
comparability
    ABCe standards and, 102
    basis of IFABC standardization, 34
    context dependence and, 160
    limitations of page impressions for, 91
completion rates
    complexity of calculation, 127, 129
    measuring for key processes, eBay.com, 113
    selling flow redesign effects on, 131
connection methods, home and business internet
    use, 93
content appealing to subscribers and non-
    subscribers, 158

Q

qryAppendCookies, 49
    querying for unique cookie visitors, 58
qryAppendLinkClickThroughs, 53
qryAppendPageViews, 50
qryAppendReferers, 52
qryDeleteLogsContent, 53
qryPageViewsByCategory, 55
    Pivot Tables and, 57
qryReferrerByDate, 54
queries, database log analysis, 54-58
query strings
    identifying affiliate scheme members, 156
    server log file recording, 16
    session management using, 146

R

random sampling
    ASPToday.com traffic reports, 150
    eBay.com use of JavaScript, 121
    NetGenesis output, 103
Randomize function, ASP, 40
reach of a web site
    assessing with panel surveys, 12
    BBC News Online use, 92
RedSherrif tagging solutions provider, 88, 93
referers (sic)
    adding to the log database, 52
    finding the most frequent referrer, 54
    identifying in Analog reports, 25
    server log file recording, 17
refreshing queries inserted into Excel, 56
registration
    allowing cookies to identify individuals, 62
    information source, ASPToday.com, 142
regular visitor identification, ASPToday.com, 150
Replace function, ASP, 41
reports
    ASPToday.com web site, 149
    BBC News Online web site, 94-103
        Analog analysis tool, 100

    audited log analysis, 99
    detailed visitor analysis, 101
    NetGenesis sample output, 102
    page impressions daily breakdown, 97, 98
eBay.com site
    page flow analysis, 117
    page property reports, 119
    page view reports, 115
    technographic reports, 118
    unique visitor reports, 116
requirements specification, eBay.com traffic analysis
    system, 115
Rnd function, ASP, 41
robots
    ABCe exclusion criteria, 98, 102
    distinguished by JavaScript, 121
    excluding from Analog reports, 23, 100
    excluding from BBC league table generator, 95
    excluding from I/Pro reports, 78
    filtering from log database imports, 50
    source of noise in log files, 10
        ASPToday.com web site, 143
ROI (Return On Investment), 113, 157
rules of traffic analysis, 36

S

Safe Harbor privacy framework, 66
screen resolution, 118
scripts
    see also JavaScript.
    BBC league table generator, 95
    setting a cookie token, 40
Seal Programs, 68
    NYTimes.com web site and, 82
search engines, identifying in Analog reports, 24
search functionality, ASPToday.com
    affiliate scheme, 156
    changes affect page impressions, 144
    tailoring to users needs, 155
search pages, eBay.com next page reports, 117
searching with keywords, eBay.com site, 114, 132
    search results page, 132
seller's other items feature, eBay.com, 134

T

Notes

Notes

Notes

Notes

glasshaus

web professional to web professional

glasshaus writes books for you. Any suggestions, or ideas about how you want
information given in your ideal book will be studied by our team.
Your comments are always valued at glasshaus.

Free phone in USA 800-873 9769
Fax (312) 893 8001

UK Tel.: (0121) 687 4100   Fax: (0121) 687 4101

Practical Web Traffic Analysis – Registration Card

Name _____

Address _____

_____

_____

City _____ State/Region_____

Country _____ Postcode/Zip_____

E-Mail _____

Occupation _____

How did you hear about this book?

❏ Book review (name) _____

❏ Advertisement (name) _____

❏ Recommendation _____

❏ Catalog _____

❏ Other _____

Where did you buy this book?

❏ Bookstore (name) _____ City_____

❏ Computer store (name) _____

❏ Mail order _____

❏ Other _____

What influenced you in the purchase of this book?

❏ Cover Design ❏ Contents ❏ Other (please specify):

_____

How did you rate the overall content of this book?

❏ Excellent ❏ Good ❏ Average ❏ Poor

What did you find most useful about this book? _____

_____

What did you find least useful about this book? _____

_____

_____

Please add any additional comments. _____

_____

_____

What other subjects will you buy a computer book on soon?

_____

What is the best computer book you have used this year?

Note: This information will only be used to keep you updated
about new glasshaus titles and will not be used for
any other purpose or passed to any other third party.

glasshaus

web professional to web professional

Note: If you post the bounce back card below in the UK, please send it to:

glasshaus, Arden House, 1102 Warwick Road,
Acocks Green, Birmingham B27 6HB. UK.

Computer Book Publishers

BUSINESS REPLY MAIL

FIRST CLASS MAIL   PERMIT#64   CHICAGO, IL

POSTAGE WILL BE PAID BY ADDRESSEE

glasshaus
29 S. LA SALLE ST.,
SUITE 520
CHICAGO IL 60603-USA